AGED OUT

AGED OUT

Narratives of Young Women
Who Grew Up in Out-of-Home Care

DR. LANETTA N. GREER

ARCHWAY PUBLISHING

Archway Publishing books may be ordered through booksellers or by contacting:

Archway Publishing
1663 Liberty Drive
Bloomington, IN 47403
www.archwaypublishing.com
1 (888) 242-5904

Because of the dynamic nature of the Internet, any web addresses or
links contained in this book may have changed since publication and
may no longer be valid. The views expressed in this work are solely those
of the author and do not necessarily reflect the views of the publisher,
and the publisher hereby disclaims any responsibility for them.

Any people depicted in stock imagery provided by Getty Images are
models, and such images are being used for illustrative purposes only.
Certain stock imagery © Getty Images.

ISBN: 978-1-4808-7998-0 (sc)
ISBN: 978-1-4808-7997-3 (hc)
ISBN: 978-1-4808-7999-7 (e)

Library of Congress Control Number: 2020907450

Print information available on the last page.

Archway Publishing rev. date: 04/25/2020

ABSTRACT

Aged Out: Narratives of Young Women
who Grew up in Out-of-Home Care

Dr. Lanetta N. Greer

This is a qualitative study involving young women who aged out of out-of-home care (OHC). Narrative inquiry will be the research methodology. Research questions will be centered on the participants' description of their family life, growing up in OHC, and life after aging out. The results of the study will better inform service providers working with youth in foster/group homes, schools, juvenile justice placements, and community programs, offering them more effective ways of assisting, supporting, and advocating for youth to ensure a more successful transition to independence after aging out.

CONTENTS

LIST OF FIGURES

Figure 1
Figure 1: Participants' data is organized by age at detainment (initial placement in OHC), number of foster homes, number of group homes, and age at discharge.

Figure 2
Figure 2: Participants data is organized by race, birthplace, reason for detainment, if reentry in OHC after attempt at reunification, whether or not they had a job, graduated from high school, have been to jail, been pregnant, been homeless, and what they miss the most and least about OHC.

CHAPTER 1

Introduction

"EACH YEAR IN THE UNITED STATES, MORE THAN 250,000 children are physically harmed or neglected by their caretakers, and enter out-of-home care" (*The AFCARS Report*, November 2013). It has long been recognized that parents have a fundamental liberty (protected by the constitution) to raise their children as they choose. As guided by federal statutes, the legal framework regarding the parent-child relationship balances the rights and responsibilities among the parents, the child, and the state. This parent-child relationship identifies certain rights, duties, and obligations, including the responsibility of the parents to protect the child's safety and well-being. If parents, however, are unable or unwilling to meet this responsibility, the state has the power and authority to act to protect the child from harm.

The basis for government intervention in child maltreatment is grounded in the concept of *parens patriae,* a legal term that asserts government has a role in protecting the interests of children and in intervening when parents fail to provide proper care. Child protective services (CPS) intervention in the United

States is based on the principle that protecting children is justified only if the bodily integrity, health, and sustenance needs of the child are jeopardized (i.e., bruises, burns, malnutrition, or other physical harm that is evident; Pecora and Whitaker, 2000). It assumes children are best served by government programs that, at minimum, ensure the safety, permanence, and well-being the state sees necessary to become productive citizens. While there are programs designed for families that can remain together (intensive in-home services), other situations, because of safety concerns, do sometimes require emergency removal of the child by a social worker from the biological family. This is referred to as placement in out-of-home care (OHC). Types of OHC placements include shelters, assessment centers, foster homes, treatment foster homes, group foster homes, and residential care centers.

Children in OHC

Although it might seem logical to expect that children in foster care would welcome a home free of abuse and neglect, they often suffer because of separation from their parents. Doyle (1990) suggests the abused child looks at removal from the home from three perspectives—the child as a family member with strong blood ties, the child as a victim (i.e., hostage and kidnap victims), and the child as a victim with an abundance of unsettling emotions. She defines this pattern as the Stockholm syndrome. The removed child goes from denial that the biological parents truly intend harm to fear and anger against the rescuing authorities and finally to gratitude toward the abusing parent. She acknowledges, "Many other youngsters, even those who have been seriously abused, defend their parents, hide their injuries, guard the family secret and try to avoid removal from home." Doyle refers to this phenomenon as "the paradox of the victim who *resists rescue*" (p. 252).

Rockhill (2010) argues, "As soon as a child *is placed* in an institution, the role of the state in regulating the relationship between itself and the parents, increases considerably. Although this might still look like cooperation, the power balance starts tipping, at first unnoticeably, until some parents become completely overwhelmed by the state" (p. 87). Parent responses range from compliance to rebellion depending on the sometimes overwhelming expectations of the court for their kids to be returned home. Parents and children often express confusion and frustration as to what and how long it will be until they return home. In addition, they must wait for social workers and the courts to make decisions in their best interests.

Surprisingly, despite the CPS goal of child well-being, research shows children placed in OHC have negative life outcomes. The National Research Council (1993), via its Panel on High-Risk Youth, concludes that "adolescents who pass through the child welfare system are at high risk of educational failure, unemployment, emotional disturbance, and other negative outcomes ... Adolescents released from foster care fare far worse than either low-income youths or a cross section of the general population" (p. 4). The panel argues that the lack of daily intimate contact with a caregiver causes somewhat of a constant disconnect. Unfortunately, normal daily relationships and activities with supportive caregivers are not always possible for youth in OHC. Such relationships usually depend on the placement(s), including staff turnover and funding issues. The ultimate factor is that on or about the age of eighteen, wards are discharged from state care. They are often without resources or any feasible transitional living plan.

Statement of the Problem: Aging Out of OHC

Rarely is this transition to independence successful for any youth, especially those who spent most of their lives in OHC. In general, young adults continue to depend on their parents even if they have gone to college, moved out, and started families of their own. For young adults previously in OHC, this is rarely the case. Family bonds have been broken because of the separation; the children and their parents harbor resentment for different reasons. Social bonds have been broken because of the constant changes in placements, schools, and caregivers while growing up in OHC. These circumstances result in many of these young people searching for some level of stability in their adult lives.

The transition to adulthood for all youth has become increasingly complex. During this period, young people cycle between attending school, working, and living independently. Many youth can rely on their families for financial and emotional support during the transition. "On average, parents give their children an estimated $38,000—or about $2,200 a year—between the ages of 18 and 34 to supplement wages, pay for college tuition, and help with housing costs, among other types of financial assistance" (Schoeni and Ross, 2005). Parents also allow their adult children to live with them and provide their children with nonmaterial assistance, such as help with obtaining a driver's license, guidance on applying to college, advice on finances and establishing a new household, and connections to other caring adults in their communities.

Census data indicate youth in the general population leave the parental home at age twenty-three and often return home after an initial stalled attempt at living independently (Williams, 2005). The average age children in the general population finally depart the home is twenty-eight (Clark and Davis, 2005). Not only are children leaving home later, but a pattern of successive returns to the parental home by youth (in general) after leaving is significant (Baum and Ma, 2007). Developmentally, this stage of life, recently termed emerging adulthood, occurs roughly between the ages of eighteen and twenty-five. It has been characterized as stressful and filled with uncertainty (Arnett, 2000). In today's culture, scholars have argued young adults in this "boomerang generation" receive more help from their parents than those in past generations (Furstenberg, Rumbaut, and Settersten, 2005).

Children may be in an OHC placement until they turn eighteen or nineteen if they are still attending high school. "Aging out" of OHC is defined as being at the end of a placement with no subsequent placement decisions made by an agency or the court. In these instances, a child exits a placement, and the child welfare agency is no longer responsible for his or her physical custody. The most current federal data indicate that more than twenty-three thousand youth between the ages of eighteen and twenty-one aged out of the foster care system in 2012 (*The AFCARS Report*, November 2013). They had few resources and little support. Their data suggest the following factors contribute to an unsuccessful transition: limited education, unemployment, incarceration, homelessness, substance abuse, unwanted pregnancy, and inadequate health care.

In addition to being asked to find an alternative living situation at the age of eighteen, youth aging out of care are abruptly forced to find all new service providers—schools, jobs, mental health providers, doctors, and transportation closer to their new homes (which may or may not be permanent). On exiting the foster care system, a significant number of youth experience hardships and struggles, including homelessness (Courtney, Piliavin, Grogan-Kaylor, and Nesmith, 2001), unemployment (Cook, 1994), incarceration (Barth, 1990), and difficulties with health and mental health concerns and limited health care coverage (Barth, 1990).

A consistent finding is that youth in foster care are more likely to drop out of school than those who have not been in care (Courtney et al., 2001). Again, most of the explanation for these differences is that youth in OHC move from placement to placement and school to school, making it impossible to develop long-term relationships with caregivers and teachers. The supportive roles fulfilled by the family, the peer group, the school, and the community predict positive outcomes for children (Rosenfeld, Richman, and Bowen, 2000). Eighty percent of children change schools when they change out-of-home placements (Berrick, Courtney, and Barth, 1993), which strains their ability to perform at the same level as other students.

In 1999, the Division of Children and Family Services, in collaboration with the University of Wisconsin-Madison School of Social Work, established the Independent Living Advisory Committee. The role of the committee was to determine the needs of these youth and to provide recommendations as to how the current child welfare system can achieve measurable improvements. The mission of the Independent Living Advisory Committee, reflecting its belief that these are "our children," is to assure that all youth exiting the OHC system in Wisconsin will make the transition to adulthood as self-sufficient, productive, and healthy individuals.

In terms of the youth who are specifically served with federal independent living funds, the committee report emphasized consideration of the following groups in the priority listed:

1. youth who exited care on their eighteen birthday and who were in OHC for at least two years prior to their exits,
2. youth who exited care between their seventeenth and eighteenth birthdays and who were in care for at least two years prior to their exits,

3. youth who exited care after the age of seventeen and who were in care for at least one year, and
4. all other youth who exit the OHC system.

The goal is for all youth aged sixteen or older exiting out-of-home care to leave care with a minimum of the following:

- driver's license or preparation for obtaining a driver's license or other access to transportation to school, employment, and other critical activities;
- high school diploma or GED or enrollment in an educational program designed to result in a high school diploma or GED;
- written employment history;
- copies of their birth certificate, social security card, and medical records;
- access to funds adequate to support him or herself for a period of three months following exit from care;
- access to and knowledge of local resources, including but not limited to food pantries, human service agencies, health clinics, and mental health facilities; and
- a safe and stable living environment.

—WI Independent Living Advisory Report, 1999

The committee's conclusion was that targeting these particular areas would create better outcomes for youth in out-of-home care (i.e. secure housing, employment, education, and income). Unfortunately, these youth face several barriers to becoming self-sufficient. In order to narrow the disadvantages, we need to understand how youth experience OHC and how they make meaning of those experiences.

Purpose of the Study

This study proposes a qualitative approach to gather the narratives of women who have aged out of OHC. Research questions will be centered on the participant's description of her life—feelings, knowledge, and behavior—at three points in time, namely family life, growing up in out-of-home care, and life after aging out. Children in need of protection services face the dilemma of loyalty to their biological family and acceptance of rescuing authorities. Children placed in OHC face additional challenges starting with the separation from their biological family, moving from one OHC placement to another, and ultimately aging out with little resources and support.

My goal is that the results of the study will help service providers assist and support youth in out-of-home care. Specifically, I hope this information can assist in creating better outcomes for youth aging out of OHC (i.e., more adequate shelter, educational attainment, employment/employment stability, healthy relationships, and financial independence). Through their stories we see their struggles and survival. This research offers insight for child-placing agencies, policy makers, mental health professionals, educators, youth care workers, and all youth.

There are several areas of literature that were relevant to this study. For example, consider the history of child maltreatment (where did the earliest cases come from, who reported the maltreatment or abuse, and what was done to the abusing parent or caregiver). Second, what other policies grew from this issue, and why did those policies change over time. Finally, how does government involvement affect outcomes of youth in out-of-home care? What policies needed to change in order for the outcomes to be better for foster youth as they prepared for their transition to independence?

CHAPTER 2

Review of the Literature

Maltreatment of Children: A Historical Perspective

BEFORE CHILD WELFARE LAWS WERE DEVELOPED, PARents and guardians were able to treat their children as they saw appropriate. "Maltreatment of children has been justified for centuries by the belief that severe physical punishment was necessary to maintain discipline, to transmit educational ideas, to please certain gods or to expel evil spirits" (Radbill, 1968). Children have been abused, neglected, and abandoned by their parents and other caregivers for centuries.

As early as 1735, the American colonies passed laws that allowed abandoned or neglected children to be "bound out" to another family as workers. The primary goal was to reduce crime by unsupervised youth and help these youth to learn some sort of trade. Shultz (1924) cites one of the earliest cases of maltreatment. The Department of Charities placed an eighteen-month-old with a family to work until she was eighteen. When the agency finally came out to the home to investigate Mary Ellen, who was subject to regular beatings, she was covered with bruises and suffering from a cut near the eye. But no action was taken because child abuse was not against the law.

A neighbor convinced the Society for the Prevention of Cruelty to Animals to instigate action in Mary Ellen's case, and that organization launched an investigation. Mary Ellen testified against the foster parents, and as a result, the foster mother was sentenced to one year in jail for assault. Mary Ellen, then an eight-year-old abuse victim, was placed in an asylum for delinquents called "Sheltering Arms." The Department of Charities had several hundred children in this same situation because social workers never checked to see how the children were doing. Their explanation was that the indentured contracts only required foster parents to report on the ward once a year.

As a result of the case of Mary Ellen, societies for the prevention of cruelty to children were formed. The New York Society for the Prevention of Cruelty to Children (SPCC) was established in December 1874. "The organization was given almost unlimited power to seek out and rescue from the dens and slums of the city the little unfortunates whose childish lives are rendered miserable by the constant abuse and cruelties practiced on them by the human brutes who happen to possess the custody or control of them" and "to enforce by lawful means and with energy the laws referred to (for the protection of children), and secure in like manner the prompt conviction and punishment of every violator of any of these laws" (Shultz, 1924, p.163). In April 1875, the New York SPCC was incorporated and empowered to bring a complaint before any court or magistrate of any violation of laws affecting children. In May 1875, the society prosecuted its first case, and in April 1876, the New York legislature introduced and passed a law "to Prevent and Punish Wrongs to Children"

(Shultz, 1924, p. 163). States and local jurisdictions started initiating mechanisms to assist and protect children. In 1912, the federal government established the Children's Bureau to guide federal programs that were designed to support state child welfare programs as well as to direct federal aid to families. In 1922, there were fifty-seven societies for the prevention of cruelty to children.

Public Policy Frameworks in the United States regarding Child Maltreatment

One of the oldest pieces of child welfare legislation, Title IV-E of the Social Security Act (1935), created the largest funding source for services to children in the foster care system. Included in the Social Security Act are payments to foster parents and funds for training for foster care providers and child welfare staff. The addition of Title XX gave states and local governments much more power over spending in the area of social services.

In 1946 in New York City, Dr. John Caffey noted in X-rays of children evaluated for "falls" that the children were being repeatedly subject to trauma and suggested that it was intentional. However, it was not until seven years later that his colleagues agreed with the diagnosis of child abuse. In 1959, the General Assembly of the United States of the United Nations adopted the Declaration of the Rights of the Child, stating that each child should be allowed a normal development and receive help, relief, and protection in times of distress. The assumption was that children are not competent to make decisions for themselves and that therefore, others (i.e., the government) should intervene to act in their *best interests*.

There were still concerns about lengthy stays children were experiencing in foster care. Henry Maas and Richard Engler

(1959) reported the first call against "foster care drift." They found that once children have been in foster care for at least eighteen months, they are likely to remain in care without being returned home or placed in another permanent home. Their findings suggest that a number of factors (e.g., ethnicity, time in care, parental visiting, region of placement, and reason for placement) are related to the probability that a child will return home. The alternative is that most children are likely to "grow up" in foster care (p. 421).

According to Hawes (1991), the modern children's rights movement emerged in the 1960s. This movement produced greater awareness of child maltreatment, the passage of national legislation aimed at improving the lives of children, significant court rulings, and the emergence of a number of child advocacy groups. The underlying concern of policy makers was still the notion of foster care *drift*, which included the long lengths of stays in out-of-home care and the multiple placements. The conclusion was that children were trapped in foster care and constantly moving from one placement to another (Usher et al., 1999).

In 1961, the American Academy of Pediatrics alerted its members to the prevalence of the "battered child syndrome." This act puts the nation on notice of the existence of the problem (Nazario, 1988). In 1962, C. Henry Kempe and his colleagues, who had been studying abuse and neglect in young children for more than a decade, had discovered that not only was child abuse a larger problem than most people knew but also that nobody was really responsible for reporting or preventing it.

By 1971, every state had laws requiring that suspected incidents of child abuse be reported to designated child protection agencies. Congress has passed significant pieces of legislation that support the states' duty and power to act on behalf of children when parents are unable or unwilling to do so. The Child

Abuse Prevention and Treatment Act (CAPTA) is one of the key pieces of legislation that guides child protection. CAPTA, in its original inception, was signed into law in 1974 (The Child Abuse Prevention Act Public Law 93-247, 1974).

This act authorized $15,000,000 in 1974, $20,000,000 in 1978, and $25,000,000 in 1976 (and for the following year) in funding for an advisory board on child abuse and neglect that was composed of representatives from federal agencies to assist the secretary in coordinating programs and activities related to child abuse and neglect. The advisory board also assisted the secretary in the development of federal standards for child abuse and neglect prevention and treatment programs.

This act established an office to be known as the National Center on Child Abuse and Neglect, which would compile, analyze, and publish a summary annually of recently conducted and currently conducted research on child abuse and neglect. Second, it would develop and maintain information on all programs, including private programs, showing promise of success in the prevention, identification, and treatment of child abuse and neglect. Third, it would compile and publish training materials for personnel and provide technical assistance (directly or through grants or contracts) to public and nonprofit private agencies and organizations to assist them in planning, improving, developing, and carrying out programs and activities relating to the prevention, identification, and treatment of child abuse and neglect. Finally, it would conduct research into the causes of child abuse and neglect, its prevention, identification, and treatment, and make a complete and full study (The Child Abuse Prevention Act Public Law 93-247, 1974).

CAPTA defines "child abuse and neglect" as the physical, mental, or sexual abuse and negligent or maltreatment of a child under the age of eighteen by a person who is responsible for the child's welfare. The CAPTA legislation was passed in response to public concern about the abuse of children—concern that was stimulated in part by the publicizing of the "battered child syndrome." The purpose of the act was to "provide financial assistance for demonstration programs for the prevention, identification, and treatment of child abuse and neglect, and to establish a National Center on Child Abuse and Neglect" (Child Abuse Prevention and Treatment Act Report, 1974). "This Act has been considered problematic because of problems in reporting laws, underdeveloped risk assessment technology, too broad a scope of intervention, insufficient funding, lack of worker training, poor program design, lack of adequate intervention research, and other issues" (Pecora et al., 2000, p. 6).

Because of the large number of Indian children being removed from their biological home, Congress enacted the Indian Child Welfare Act (ICWA) in 1978, finding that "there is no resource more vital to the continued existence and integrity of the Indian Tribe than their children" and "an alarming high percentage of Indian families are broken up by the removal, often unwarranted, of their children ... by nontribal public and private agencies" (Pecora et al., 2000, p. 4). The ICWA creates procedural safeguards in matters pertaining to custody and placement of Indian children. "Full faith and credit" must be given to the judgments of tribal courts over child welfare cases. According to the act, state jurisdiction over child custody hearings can be transferred to the tribe. The act specifies placements and preferences for states in placing Indian children in foster or adoptive homes. Tribal governments may legislate their own preferences and state courts ordinarily follow them.

The Federal Adoption Assistance and Child Welfare Act of 1980 was an outgrowth of child welfare reform in California and other states (Ten Broeck and Barth, 1986). The law restructured and expanded the child welfare system in California. Four child welfare service programs were established—emergency response, family maintenance, family reunification, and permanency planning. The goals were to prevent unnecessary foster care placements, to reunify with biological parents whenever possible, to reduce long-term foster care placements, and to assure stable and family-like placements for those in foster care (State of California Legislative Analyst Office, 1985).

There was continued discussion surrounding how OHC affected children. Knitzer's (1982) monograph, "Unclaimed Children: The Failure of Public Responsibility to Children and Adolescents in Need of Mental Health Services," led to the national Child and Adolescent Service System Program (CASSP), which was based on principles designed to better integrate child and youth services across service sectors. In 1982, Knitzer issued a clarion critique of the mental health service system in the United States, arguing that many children in need of these services were not even being identified because they were involved with other service systems (e.g., child welfare and juvenile justice). Klee and Halfon (1987) published a study on "Mental Health Care for Foster Children in California," finding that only one among fourteen counties examined provided routine mental health evaluations for children in foster care settings. Klee and Halfon's findings were early critical indicators of the need to examine the mental health care of children involved with the child welfare system.

As a result of a debate on welfare reform in 1995–96 between Republicans and then Senator Daniel Patrick Moynihan, $6 million per year for seven years was given to conduct a national survey of children in the child protection system. The text of the legislation, which passed as part of the 1996 welfare reform, instructed the Department of Health and Human Services to conduct a study that followed children in the child protection system for several years to discover how their cases were handled by the system, whether they were removed from their homes, what types of services they and their parents received, what their developmental outcomes were, and whether measures of the way cases were handled and services obtained were related to developmental outcomes (Haskins et al., 2007). The goals were to provide an overall picture of how the nation's child protection system works and to highlight child outcomes (i.e., to preserve child safety and to achieve permanent placements whether with family or adoption).

Congress approved the study for two reasons—to know whether the placements of children and the services they received influenced their growth and development and to appease members of Congress who wanted reliable data for the nation as a whole and for as many states as possible.

The Adoption and Safe Families Act (ASFA, 1997) shortened the time frame for permanency decisions from eighteen to twelve months after foster care entry, mandated initiation of termination of parental rights for children in care for fifteen of the previous twenty-two months, emphasized the safety of foster care children in foster care, excluded long-term foster care as a permanency option, identified unreasonable situations for reunification, and provided monetary incentives to states for adoption. The Promoting Safe and Stable Families Act (1997) authorized funding for services to reunify foster children with their birth parents, to promote and support adoption of foster children, and to improve court systems responsible for monitoring permanency for foster children.

The ASFA established that, in addition to reunification, adoption, placement with a relative, and legal guardianship, "another planned permanent living arrangement" (APPLA) is specified as a permanency option and may include independent living. Section 477 of the act encourages states to continue their efforts to achieve permanency for a young person, including by specifying that states should continue to locate and achieve placement in adoptive families for older youth in care. In his introductory remarks about the Senate version of P. L. 106-169 (S. 1327), Senator Jay Rockefeller described the intent of the legislation,

> [A] Youth's need for a family does not end at any particular age. Each of us can clearly recall times when we have had to turn to our own families for advice, comfort, or support long after our 18th or 21st birthdays. Many of us are still in the role of providing such support to our own children who are in their late teens or 20s. Therefore, an important provision in this Senate version of the Foster Care Independence Act states that Independent Living (IL) programs are not alternatives to permanency planning—young people of all ages need and deserve every possible effort made towards permanence, including adoption. It would be counterproductive to create any disincentive for adoption of teenagers. (Fernandes, 2008, p. 23)

In 2003, CAPTA was reauthorized and amended by the Keeping Children and Families Safe Act. The CAPTA Reauthorization 2010 was signed under the Obama administration. The act recognizes the diversity of ethnic, cultural, and religious beliefs that may impact childrearing. Second, it recognizes that both child maltreatment and domestic violence occur in up to 60 percent of the families where either is present. Also, it develops effective approaches that improve the relationship and attachment of infants and toddlers who experience abuse or neglect from their parents or primary caregivers. Finally, it authorizes the collection of better data of perpetrators involved in the shaken baby syndrome and characteristics of victims (The CAPTA Reauthorization Act Public Law 111-320, 2010).

Public Policy in the United States regarding Aging Out

In the child welfare community, focus is increasing on the transition of youth out of care at age eighteen or older, many of whom had entered care in their early teens. Each year about twenty-five thousand youth exit care in this way (Administration for Children and Families, 2008). The sudden transition from foster care to independent living status is difficult for most foster youth, but those youth who also seek to continue their education or training may find additional demands (Sim, Emerson, O'Brien, Pecora, and Silva, 2008). One reason for this is foster youth may lose supportive adults they had while in OHC, such as caregivers, educators, mentors, employers, social workers, and mental health providers.

Being in care may actually cause instability because of multiple out-of-home placements, school transfers, and the challenge in maintaining relationships with parents and other relatives. Youth may experience further instability if they cannot afford to live on their own or are unable to live with relatives or friends upon discharge. For older foster youth and those who have already aged out of care, assistance is often not in place.

Not surprisingly, the number of foster youth proceeding to postsecondary education is low, despite evidence that suggests a college degree is more important now than ever for employability. For those who do attend college, only 26 percent who enter college finish their degrees in six years as opposed to a 56 percent completion rate among other undergraduates (Snyder and Tan, 2006). Former foster youth report that financial problems, especially during crises, are a major reason they must stop attending school. Transportation is often another factor.

Adolescents who have received child welfare services exhibit more delinquency and fewer social skills than youth in the general population (Wall, Barth, and the NSCAW Research Group, 2005).

Recognizing the difficulties faced by older youth in care and youth leaving foster care, Congress created an Independent Living Initiative to assist certain older foster youth as they enter adulthood. The Federal Independent Living Program (ILP) was first authorized in 1986 through the addition of section 477 to Title IV-E of the Social Security Act. The ILP was initiated to enable child welfare agencies to respond to the needs of youth transitioning from foster care and assist them as they prepare for independent living.

Independent living programs are intended to assist youth in preparing for adulthood, and they may include assistance in obtaining a high school diploma, career exploration, training in daily living skills, training in budgeting and financial management skills, and preventive health activities, among other services. Further, the act required states to provide services to tribal youth on the same basis as other youth in the state. Most importantly, the act encourages youth in foster care to participate directly in designing their own activities that prepare them for independent living and further states that youth need to "accept personal responsibility for living up to their part of the program" (The Federal Independent Living Program [ILP] Public Law 99-272, 1986).

A permanency hearing for a youth transitioning from foster care to a planned permanent living arrangement or independent living is held in a family or juvenile court or another court, including a tribal court. H.R. 3409 and H.R. 4208/S. 2560 specify that where appropriate, the state is to include in the written case plan for a child who is fourteen years old in care a description of the programs and services that will facilitate his or her transition from foster care to independent living. The plan must discuss the appropriateness of the services that have been provided to the child and document the steps the agency is taking to find a permanent placement with a family or other adult connection for the youth as well as a permanent living arrangement. In addition, the bill requires that the permanency hearing review all documentation of the efforts to secure a permanent living arrangement for the child upon emancipating. It further requires that the state inform all children leaving care of the full range of available financial, housing, counseling, health, and other services for which the youth is eligible and also teach them how to access the services under these programs.

The Foster Care Independence Act of 1999 focused on the needs of adolescents transitioning out of foster care by doubling the funds to pay for the board and maintenance of eighteen- to twenty-one-year-old foster youth and the preparation for foster parents to provide care for them. This legislation also authorized funds for programs that facilitate these youths' independence as well as a variety of support services (e.g., housing, education, and health care). This policy meets the unique needs of older adolescents in care, even beyond independent living goals. It also gives states the option to extend Medicaid to these older youth transitioning from foster care. The name was changed to the John H. Chafee Foster Care Independence Program as a testimonial to Senator Chafee's long-standing leadership for children in foster care.

The 1999 Foster Care Independence Act doubled the annual funds available to states for independent living services from $70 million to $140 million. To be eligible for funds, the act requires states to expand the population of youth who receive independent living services to include those who have aged out of foster care until their twenty-first birthday and those of any age in foster care who are expected to leave care without placement in a permanent family. Services may consist of educational assistance, vocational training, mentoring, preventive health activities, and counseling. States may dedicate as much as 30 percent of their program funding toward room and board for youth ages eighteen to twenty-one, including youth enrolled in an institution of higher education or who remain in foster care in states that provide care to youth until ages nineteen, twenty, or twenty-one. Room and board are not defined in statute, but typically include food and shelter and may include rental deposits, rent, utilities, and the cost of household startup purchases.

Examples of Other States' Policies and Practice regarding Aging Out

Although more than half of all states report that youth remain in foster care custody under certain circumstances until at least age twenty-one, a much smaller number of states appear to encourage youth to do so. This is evidenced by the small number of youth ages eighteen through twenty in foster care, as reported by HHS's Adoption and Foster Care Reporting and Analysis System (AFCARS), the federal system that collects national foster care data. Data from AFCARS in November 2013 (the most recent year data) illustrates a significant drop off between the number of youth age seventeen (29,288; 7 percent of the foster care population) compared to youth age eighteen (11,280; 3 percent); age nineteen (3,588; 1 percent); and age twenty (2,448; 1 percent).

The Congressional Research Service contacted four jurisdictions—Illinois, New York, Vermont, and Washington, DC— that are known to retain youth in foster care from age eighteen to twenty-one or twenty-two. These jurisdictions provide state foster care maintenance payments to fund foster care for older youth and may use other funds besides Title IV-E maintenance payments. The four foster care programs for youth ages eighteen and older vary. While Illinois, New York, and Washington, DC, provide more traditional foster care maintenance payments to foster families on behalf of youth ages eighteen to twenty-one, Vermont provides stipends (much like foster care maintenance payments) to caring adults (including foster care families) who pledge to assist youth who have aged out of care.

In Washington, DC, youth *must remain in care* until their twenty-first birthday unless they meet narrow criteria, whereas in Illinois and New York, eligible youth may decide to seek emancipation before reaching age twenty-one. Former foster youth in Vermont are not required to participate in the program. Further, New York and Vermont require youth to be enrolled in an educational or workforce program as a condition for remaining in care; Illinois and Washington, DC, do not. In all cases, with the exception of Vermont, youth ages eighteen and older in care continue to be wards of the state. The juvenile courts retain jurisdiction and social workers make routine visits to assist youth in achieving their case goal, which is often independent living or another planned living arrangement (US Department of Health and Human Services AFCARS Report 14, 2006).

States have flexible funding to provide those children who are identified as likely to remain in foster care until age eighteen with a plan and services, including (a) to receive the education, training, and services necessary to obtain employment; (b) to prepare for postsecondary education; and (c) to be mentored. The minimum eligibility age of sixteen, as adopted in the Independent Living Initiative of 1986, has been removed. All states are now eligible for a minimum of $500,000, but states must provide a 20 percent match for the entire amount. States are given the option of extending Medicaid to youths eighteen to twenty-one who have left foster care. The asset limit under which youths in foster care remain eligible for Aid to Families with Dependent Children (AFDC) and thereby maintain eligibility for Title IV-E Foster Care Assistance increased from $1,000 to $10,000 (The Foster Care Independence Act Public Law 106-169, 1999).

The US Department of Health and Human Services (HHS) in consultation with federal, state, and local officials, advocates, youth service providers, and researchers has developed outcome measures to assess state performance. Outcomes include educational attainment, employment, avoidance of dependency, homelessness, nonmarital childbirth, high-risk behaviors, and incarceration. HHS must report to Congress and propose state accountability procedures and penalties for noncompliance. States must seek wide private and public sector input into the development of their five-year IL plan, and interested public members must have at least thirty days to comment on the plan. Each Indian tribe in the state shall be consulted about the state's IL programs, and the programs must be as available for Indian children as they are for other children in the state. States must attempt to coordinate their IL programs with other state and federally funded programs for youth (especially JJDPA transitional living funds) and with abstinence education programs, local housing programs, programs for disabled youth (especially sheltered youth workshops), and school-to-work programs offered through high schools or local workforce agencies. States are required to use Title IV-E training funds to train adoptive and foster parents, workers in group homes, and case managers to help them address the issues confronting adolescents preparing for independent living (Administration for Children and Families AFCARS Report 14, 2008).

The Workforce Investment Act (WIA) authorizes job training programs for unemployed and underemployed individuals through the Department of Labor (DOL). Two of these programs—Youth Activities and Job Corps—provide job training and related services to targeted low-income vulnerable populations, including foster youth. The WIA Youth Activities program focuses on preventative strategies to help in-school youth stay in school and receive occupational skills as well as providing training and supportive services, such as assistance with child care, for out-of-school youth. Job Corps is an educational and vocational training program that helps students learn a trade, complete their GED, and secure employment. To be eligible, foster youth must meet age and income criteria as defined under the act. Young people currently or formerly in foster care may participate in Youth Activities if they are ages fourteen to twenty-one, and in Job Corps if they are ages sixteen to twenty-four (Workforce Investment Act Public Law 105-220, 1998).

Current and former foster youth may be eligible for housing services provided through programs administered by the Department of Housing and Urban Development's (HUD) family unification vouchers program (FUP vouchers). The FUP vouchers were initially created in 1990 under P.L. 101-625 for families that qualify for Section 8 tenant-based assistance and for whom the lack of adequate housing is a primary factor in the separation of children from their biological parents or in preventing the reunification of the children with their biological parents. Amendments to the program in 2000 made youth ages eighteen to twenty-one who left foster care at age sixteen or older eligible for the vouchers. These youth are eligible for the vouchers for up to eighteen months. Older current and former foster youth may also be eligible for housing services and related support through the Runaway and Homeless Youth Program, administered by the US Department of Health and Human Services. Youth transitioning out of foster care may also be eligible for select transitional living programs administered by HUD, though the programs do not specifically target these youth (Housing Choice Voucher Program Public Law 106-337, 2000).

Another related issue is temporary housing for youth in college who are unable to stay with family or friends over school breaks. One of the youth witnesses at the July 12, 2007, hearing described the difficulty in college with finding housing when her dorm was closed, "I waited in limbo for a friend to extend an invitation as I wondered where I would go for holidays and school breaks." Some states require public universities to provide housing for these youth. For example, California law requires that the California State University system and the community college system "review housing issues for those emancipated foster youth living in college dormitories to ensure basic housing during the regular academic school year, including vacations and holidays other than summer break" (California Education Code Sec. 89342, 1996).

As of July 2009, the College Cost Reduction Act allowed certain youth who have been in foster care to claim independent status when applying for federal financial aid. The act amended the definition of "independent student" in the Higher Education Act to include any child "who is an orphan, in foster care, or a ward of the court at any time when the individual is *13 years of age or older*" and "is an emancipated minor or is in legal guardianship as determined by a court of competent jurisdiction in the individual's state of legal residence." The act does not specify the length of time that the child must have been in foster care or the reason for exiting care, to be eligible to claim independent status. The law first became effective during the 2009 to 2010 school year. Students who claim independent status are typically able to access greater federal education assistance because they are exempt from including information about income and assets from their parents. An *independent* student's expected *family* contribution is the amount that the federal needs analysis system determines should be contributed based only on his or her available income (and assets if applicable) as well as basic living expenses, federal income tax liability, and other expenses (The College Cost Reduction and Access Act Public Law 110-84, 2009).

Finally, the Foster Care Mentoring Act (S. 379), permanently authorizes funding, under Title IV-B of the Social Security Act, for grants to provide mentoring to children in foster care. The grants are awarded by HHS to states or to a political subdivision of the state if it serves a "substantial number" of youth in foster care and supports, establishes, and expands networks of public and private community entities to provide this mentoring. Successful applicants are eligible to receive a maximum of $600,000 annually, are required to spend no less than 50 percent of the federal grant funds for training (and no more than 10 percent on program administration), and are to provide matching funds (in cash or in kind) of 25 percent. The bill authorized $15 million for this grant program in each of 2008 and 2009 and "such sums as may be necessary" in every following fiscal year (Mentoring Act of 2007, 110th Congress, 2009).

In this chapter, so far we see a chronological progression of child welfare law, starting with the very earliest cases of child maltreatment. There appeared to be an ongoing evaluation of the child welfare system, which caused laws to be changed and in some cases more funds to be made available for the prevention, identification, and treatment of child maltreatment. The chapter examines how services have evolved for both foster parents (e.g., more training) and foster youth (e.g., mental health assessments, permanency planning, and independent living).

Understanding Development: Attachment and Separation

In this section, I emphasize the importance of basic human development in the early stages of pregnancy and in the early ages of the child. The literature on child welfare is explained through these child development theories—drive theory, learning theory, and systems theory as they relate to attachment theory. I discuss pioneers in the field of attachment, and the connections to foster care (e.g., separation). This information is important in understanding the bond between parent and child and the barriers caregivers face when trying to support foster youth in their care.

Chouinard (2007) describes "the field of developmental psychology as having two primary goals: to describe development, and to explain development" (p. 3). Cognitive developmentalists want to identify what children and youth know at particular stages (ages) but also what it takes for their knowledge base to become more adultlike as well as what processes and abilities allow children to move from where they are to where they need to be.

Child and adolescent development is highly individualized but also a universal concept. Maier (1990) contends, "Studies of human development zero in on basic human functioning: the way a person grows and develops and what people do under various circumstances within their relevant environments" (p. 74). For Maier, development can be described by more than just behavior. It includes physical, emotional, and cognitive functioning. More specifically, development is shaped by the interactions and experiences between children/youth and their "active context." We use *normal* and *abnormal* to give insights as to how people manage their daily lives. Even though cognitive, affect, and behavior have their own distinct processes, understanding the way they engage and interact with each other can be life changing.

The importance of development is evident even before birth. Nutrition, stress, mental health, diet, prenatal care, and alcohol/drug consumption play a significant role in the development of the baby while still in the womb. Preparing the world for a baby is easy for some, yet impossible for others because of lack of education, information, and support, rendering some parents totally unable to provide basic care for their children. Ego development is anchored in the trusting relationship created through the provision of care (Maier, 1965). He describes development as a social affair, starting with the earliest interaction with people. Even as infants, babies are exploring whether the world is a safe and exciting place and whether it responds to their needs.

Other Research Surrounding Development during Infancy—The Bond between Parent and Child

Psychiatrist David Levy (1931) conducted research that focused on problematic maternal attitudes of overprotection and rejection. The emphasis was on the rehabilitation of the child's ego that had been damaged by the conscious and unconscious feelings of the parents (especially the mother) in childrearing. Soon after Levy, Ian Suttie (1935) emphasized "the need for love and companionship as an autonomous force in development, at least equal in importance to sexual instincts" (p. 210).

Spitz (1945) discussed the occurrence of *hospitalism*, the slow development and fragile health of abandoned infants who received little individual attention in group care. "Compared to the behavior of family children, for these children the unusual behavior was replaced by something that could vary from extreme friendliness to any human partner combined with anxious avoidance of inanimate objects, to a generalized anxiety expressed in blood-curdling screams which could go on indefinitely" (p. 23). Although the implications for children's emotional development were worrisome, this study provided the initial validity for the theory of attachment.

Donald Winnicott (1956) explains the maternal/paternal preoccupation as a necessary precursor for the infant's individuality to emerge. Human infants at birth are totally dependent on the caregiver to hold, carry, and provide for them. The human infant has systems in place to elicit caregiving. The infant's preference for gazing into the parent's eye and the rooting reflex serve as elicitors of care (Blauvelt, 1962). Several characteristics like big eyes and a round nose are considered cute and influence attachment. Hans Loewald (1978) points to the fact that the infant's instinctual life takes shape in the early mother-infant relationship. The overwhelming needs and dependency infants have on their parents/caregivers is just the beginning of how they make sense of the world.

Mercer (2010) states, "Marriage of a father to a child's mother has been suggested as a way to ensure the child's good development and to prevent delinquent behavior" (p. 133). One hope is in the economic sustainability of a two-parent household, and the other in the assumption that a male (father) is needed as a disciplinarian, especially for boys. However, the presence of a maltreating father can be more harmful to a child's overall development than his absence (abandonment of his family).

A Discussion of the Drive Theory, Learning Theory, and Systems Theory

Most schools of thought have their own way of conceptualizing attachment and separation. Here I will summarize several different theories—drive theory, learning theory, and systems theory—as they link to understanding development in relation to attachment and separation among children and their caregivers.

The Drive Theory

Sigmund Freud offers the first and most basic explanation of development from infancy to adulthood (Freud, 1923). Freud's interpretation, which is based on *drive theory*, explains the development of attachment between mother and infant as a result of satisfaction of the infant's oral and emotional needs through breastfeeding (Brisch, 2002). He believed that the mind of an infant consists of primitive drives and instincts (i.e., the need for food and physical comfort), which he called the id. During those first few years, the ego develops as a way for the id to be expressed. In the late preschool years, children develop a conscience (they feel guilty for misbehaving), which he referred to as the superego. Freud believed that a single motive governs human behavior—the desire to satisfy needs and remove tension.

For adolescence, Freud (1923) explores an internal struggle, the time when a child develops a balance between the ego and the id. Adolescence is also a time when the child is bombarded with instinctual impulses. Failure to experience gratification can cause a child to be *fixated* in a particular stage. For youth in out-of-home care, the number of placements (i.e., childrearing practices, nurturing/disciplining techniques, rewards systems, and overall structure/stability) will directly impact the way they progress through the stages Freud has laid out.

Many theorists in child guidance clinics have been uncomfortable with Freud's attribution of sexual impulses among children. Child guidance clinics in both England and America attributed disturbance in a child to disturbed family relations. "Social workers attached to the child guidance clinics would go into the homes and talk to the parents, looking for unconscious beliefs and wishes, feelings of guilt and disappointment, that might affect the child" (Eyer, 1992, p. 56-57). It was the mother they contacted, so her fantasies, dreams, and conflicts were those expressed. Thus maternal disturbances increasingly came to be seen as the root of children's problems. The objective was now to preserve the family.

The Learning Theory

John Bowlby believed that attachment theory was based on a behavioral-motivational system that he described as the attachment system. Bowlby was convinced that children's early experiences in relationship to their mother could play a major role in development. He refused to believe either that the Oedipus complex and its resolution or sexuality was responsible for a child's emotional development. Bowlby came from a wealthy family; his father absorbed in his profession and contact with his mother was limited to a few set hours per day. Holmes (1993) argued that "this rather distanced relationship with his mother, and the fact that he lost his most important attachment figure, his favorite nursemaid, at the age of 3, were important aspects of Bowlby's biography" (p. 7).

Bowlby was the first to recognize that childhood experiences and not just inner psychic forces affect how an individual responds, develops, and acts. He believed that the "emotional attachments of infants and toddlers to the caregivers were based on social interactions, not on physical gratification" (Mercer, 2006, p. 138). He considered early attachment experiences to have a powerful effect on personality development. He believed the quality of early attachments had two important influences on children as they grow and develop—how children relate to other people and how the child feels about him or herself. He was especially interested in the impact of attachment history on mental health and criminal behavior.

Bowlby shed light on the effect of the loss of a mother figure when he worked in a home for emotionally disturbed boys. In 1944, Bowlby published "Forty-Four Juvenile Thieves," in which he reported that many of the delinquent boys, aged five to sixteen, had suffered early maternal separation, and he concluded that these separations had been the primary cause of delinquency and affectionless psychopathy. Because the boys had no one fully committed to their well-being, many of them appeared incapable of meaningful relationships. He concluded that having a committed caregiver is crucial to children's healthy development. Otherwise, the child is vulnerable to a range of threats. From Bowlby's work, a collaborator named Mary Ainsworth developed a test-like standard procedure that she called the "Strange Situation," to study children's attachment and separation behavior in a laboratory setting (Ainsworth and Witting, 1969). The Strange Situation was developed for assessing the child's expectations of his or her parents' availability when distressed.

From the perspective of *learning theory*, it is easy to explain how children regulate closeness and distance with important attachment figures from birth onward as the result of learning procedures (i.e., reinforcement or negative consequences) (Bowlby, 1973). Bowlby's explanation was clear. During infancy and early childhood, the ego and superego are not fully operating. Children are dependent on the mother, who either permits or restricts their impulses. Continuous and satisfactory primary relationships allow the ego and superego to develop. "In this way the child is using the parent as a *secure base*, as a way of increasing feelings of security when in a situation that might arouse feelings of insecurity" (Golding, 2008, p. 83). Infants are born to form relationships where they experience security and comfort. This search for closeness may be accomplished by visual contact with the mother or close bodily contact with her. Babies are born able to elicit caregiving, and as they get older, the way they go about this becomes much more purposeful and sophisticated. Bowlby believed this process that children go through is what ultimately influences their comfort in being willing to explore new things.

Bowlby's theory of attachment supplied evidence for the role of familiar caregivers in the emotional lives of the very young. He believed that early experiences with caregivers could set a direction for good (or poor) social and emotional development. Children's attachment to their mothers or to other familiar caregivers results from a basic human motivation. It is not based on gratification of physical need, such as hunger. The infant behaviors connected with social interactions, *engagement behaviors* such as sucking, clinging, following, and signaling another person by smiling or crying, are all related to the development of attachment. They are also *inherited*, instinctual behaviors characteristic of human beings. Some of the actions that will form part of attachment behavior are already present between birth and six months of age, but they are not particularly focused on a specific one or two adults. After six months, attachment behaviors begin to be directed toward a few familiar caregivers.

Separation anxiety is an indication that attachment has occurred. When separation from familiar people is abrupt and long-lasting, however, the child who has achieved attachment is anxious and goes through stages of grieving and emotional reorganization. Attachment emotions and behavior are age-related. "Attachment behaviors and emotions are connected with the individual's internal working model of the social world" (Mercer, 2006, p. 142).

Bowlby argued that from our relationships with others, we abstract an "internal working model," which is an internal representation of ourselves, the people we have a relationship with, and the characteristics of that relationship. In other words, the quality of our attachment to the primary caregiver during infancy sets the tone and character for the relationships that we experience thereafter (Mitchell and Ziegler, 2007, p. 170). Bowlby identifies four types of attachment—secure attachment, insecure/resistant attachment, insecure/avoidant attachment, and disorganized/disoriented attachment (Mitchell and Ziegler 2007, p. 170).

Secure attachment occurs in about 50 to 67 percent of baby-caregiver relationships. Here the baby seems to treat the mother as a safe base from which to venture into unfamiliar territory. The insecure/resistance attachment is detected in about 10 percent of caregiver-baby relationships. This child tends to be clingy in the beginning of a strange situation but also tends to resist the mother when comforted. Insecure/avoidant attachment is detected in approximately 15 percent of baby-caregiver relationships. These babies are aloof. They turn away from their mothers and rarely greet them. Disorganized/disoriented attachment is also present in about 15 percent of caregiver-baby relationships. These babies behave in contradictory ways. They seem to want comfort from the mother while also feeling wary of her.

Bowlby believed that our earliest attachments impact our ability to function socially. This means that the child's early experience leads to the development of an idea/impression of how relationships work. Children learn about themselves and how others may respond from the memories of those early experiences. Children suffering from the effects of separation struggle a great deal emotionally. Bowlby proposed that "the sudden loss of a parent or sibling or of care in a succession of foster homes might cause such depression" (Eyer, 1992, p. 62).

The Systems Theory

Versions of *systems theory* claim that visible and invisible attachments develop among individual family members that control and regulate the family unit as a whole. The question is whether individuation is possible. If the development of autonomy in a child (the urge to leave home) threatens to destabilize the family as a whole, the entire family may insist on attachment loyalty, which will inhibit or prohibit the child's separation impulse (Cierpka, 1996; Stierlin, 1980). For example, in some cultures adolescents act as almost co-parents depending on the needs of the family as a whole. This can become problematic if the adolescent wants to pursue goals that may "take them away" from the family (i.e., going away to college).

Bowen family systems theory promotes an individual's opportunity for emotional growth. Two counterbalancing agents—*individuality* (separateness) and *togetherness* (fusion)—play out between members of a family (MacKay, 2012). From the Bowen perspective, child abuse is seen as an aspect of family functioning, in which there is "insufficient emotional support" between family members (Bowen, 1978). Dissociative responses develop when a person is subject to their family's severe emotional fusion.

Summary

In Bowlby's conception, the newborn does not see himself merged with the mother. As a result, the attachment between infant and caregiver must develop during the first year of life and is not a given, as argued by Freud. A variety of attachment patterns may develop in the course of this interactional process.

"Separation reactions are largely universal, no matter how close or distant the parent-child relationship might be, no matter what the type or length of the separation, and no matter if it was the first or fiftieth separation" (Klaus et al., 1995, p. 121). Any separation from the mother is important to the child. On the other hand, research suggests that children can learn self-sufficiency and independence through separation. Children may determine that other people they are entrusted to can provide care and companionship somewhat similar to that of the mother.

Attachment theory suggests the more quickly a child finds stability in an out-of-home setting, the better able that child will be to overcome early attachment failures that are associated with child maltreatment. From a practical perspective, attachment theory helps explain why disruptions in the first year of foster care are highly correlated with poor long-term outcomes. There is no consistent environment where relationships with caregivers can be nurtured.

Growing Up in Out-of-Home Care (OHC)

Who Abuses and Why?

In 2009, it was estimated that more than 80 percent of child perpetrators (persons who are involved with child abuse or maltreatment) were parents, 6.3 percent were relatives other than parents, 4.3 percent were unmarried partners of parents, 2.8 percent were unknown relationships, and 3.9 percent accounted for "other" relationships (*The BACW Bulletin*, January 2012 issue). Although specific factors may contribute to a particular type of maltreatment, it is important to examine the major theories that attempt to explain why parents and other caretakers may physically abuse, neglect, or sexually maltreat the children in their care. First, the psychiatric or psychological model views the parents' traits or upbringing as the major cause of maltreatment.

It assumes that abusive parents have certain personality characteristics that separate them from nonabusive parents (Belsky and Vondra, 1989). In this model, the abusive parent is considered mentally ill and therefore unable to provide adequate child care. Second is the sociological model, which emphasizes the social context. This model avoids "blaming the victim." Instead it focuses on cumulative environmental stresses (e.g., financial difficulties, unemployment, housing and living conditions, adolescent parenting, and poor schools) and how they relate to the family as a whole and to child maltreatment. Third, the social-situational model has also been termed the "effect of the child on the caregiver" model, in particular because this model emphasizes the role the child's own behavior plays in determining the course of the parent-child relations (Belsky and Vondra, 1989, p. 155). Particular characteristics (e.g., handicaps, mental illness, premature birth, birth defects) of the child may cause strain in the parent-child relations. In other words, "temperamental incompatibility" may be a problem. Finally, the ecological model views child abuse through the interactions of several elements—family, community, and society.

Characteristics of Children in OHC

Certain characteristics of children make them more vulnerable to foster care entry. For example, one third of children less than five years old who are placed into care are placed following a maltreatment report. With a national entry rate of 40 percent (USDHHS, 2005), adolescents are more likely to be placed in foster care than preschool kids and schoolchildren (Wulczyn and Hislop, 2002). Younger children are adopted quickly but are returned to birth families more slowly, whereas older children are returned home more quickly and adopted more slowly (Wulczyn et al., 2002).

Children of color are more likely to be placed in foster care. In 2006, 54 percent of the 295,207 children who entered foster care were children of color. Of these, 27 percent were African American, and 19 percent were Latino. In 2010, 27 percent of the 408,435 children in foster care were African American (*The BACW Bulletin*, January 2012). African American children are overrepresented in the foster care system when compared with European American children. There is considerable controversy regarding whether this disparity among races reflects the needs of the specific populations or discriminatory practices in the child welfare system (Barth, Goodhand, and Dickinson, 2000). Additionally, African American children leave foster care at a slower rate than do other children regardless of their destination after discharge (Wulczyn et al., 2002).

Poverty is another strong predictor of a child's removal from home, suggesting that the prevalence (but not necessarily the occurrence) of maltreatment is enmeshed with socioeconomic status (Lindsey, 1991). Families living below the poverty line tend to have poor nutrition and diet and higher rates of physical inactivity and to suffer more from treatable and preventable illnesses. Poverty is one factor that can impact a child's development. Studies have found that children from low-income families are "more likely to suffer from preventable illnesses, fail in school, become teenaged parents, and become involved with the justice system. As a result, these young people (similar to former foster youth) frequently reach adulthood without the necessary tools, experiences, and connections to succeed" (Annie E. Casey Foundation, 2005, p. 5). It is clear that poverty status is one of the strongest predictors of child well-being.

Foster care reentry rates are associated with race, age, and maltreatment type, and African American, older, and neglected children have the highest reentry rates (Barth et al., 2000). Additionally, children with multiple placements tend to be older and/or African American, and they may also have special needs.

The Wisconsin Experience

On December 6, 2010, the Wisconsin Department of Children and Families published an annual report for the calendar year 2009 surrounding Wisconsin children in out-of-home care. The purpose of the report is to give readers an idea of the trends found in out-of-home care. This data was gathered from the state level with information from both the Bureau of Milwaukee Child Welfare (BMCW) and Special Needs Adoption Program (SNAP).

The report begins by identifying the demographics of children placed in out-of-home care in 2009. As of December 31, 2009, a total of 6,568 children were in an OHC placement in Wisconsin. The child population (by county) of entries into out-of-home care for 2009 showed that Milwaukee County had the largest number of children (1,276). Other counties with the highest numbers include Dane County (466), Kenosha County (254), and Brown County (227). All other counties had much lower rates of entry into out-of-home care in 2009. The ages of the children statewide in OHC on December 31, 2009, were as follows. Four and under had 31 person. Five to twelve had 27 percent. Twelve to fifteen had 21 percent, and sixteen to eighteen had 21 percent.

More males are in OHC (54 percent) than females (46 percent). White children represented 52 percent of all children in OHC care. African American children represented 40 percent. Children ages sixteen to eighteen accounted for the largest share of children discharged from OHC (30 percent). Caucasian children accounted for 60 percent of total discharges from OHC, while African American children accounted for 31 percent.

The predominance of males in OHC is particularly pronounced at older ages. This pattern is due primarily to juvenile justice placements. Almost 75 percent of the 1,700 children in OHC who were identified to have a disability as of December 31, 2009, were diagnosed as emotionally disturbed. Male children spent a median time of 234 days in care before discharging. Female children spent 247 days in care. African American children appear to have significantly longer stays in care than white children (*Division of Children and Family Services/Office of program Evaluation and Planning Out of Home Care Caseload Summary Report* (r254, 3/08/07), which is based on data taken from WiSACWIS).

Public v. Private Kinship Care

Two types of kinship care exist—*public kinship care*, involving state placement of the child with relatives (often aunts/uncles), and *private kinship care*, involving informal placement from birth caregivers to kin caregivers (often grandmothers). An estimated two hundred thousand children reside in public kinship care, whereas about 2.1 million children live in private kinship care (USDHHS, 2000). Children in public kinship care tend to be younger than those in private kinship care, who also are older than children in nonrelative foster care (USDHHS, 2000). This research closely examined the experiences of children in kinship care compared to those children in nonrelative care. Kinship caregivers face more challenges with their physical health, with daily stressors and hassles, and with caring for more children. One important question is whether kin should be privileged under federal law for public assistance and foster care benefits if they are unable to meet state foster home licensing standards.

The Kinship Care Practice Project conducts research, develops training materials, and provides educational opportunities to ensure safety, well-being, and permanent homes for children through collaborative work with extended families. The project began in 1992 as a research and demonstration project funded by the Adoption Opportunities Program of the US Department of Health and Human Services Administration for Children, Youth and Families (ACYF). The project has received additional support through the Illinois Department of Children and Family Services and the Jane Addams College of Social Work.

The 1992 research project led by James Gleeson (1) examined child welfare practice with children in foster care placements with relatives and (2) developed a training curriculum and videotapes based on practice principles that promote safety, well-being, and permanent homes for children. While the kinship care practice project originally focused on families with children who are in the custody of the child welfare system, their work has expanded to include informal kinship caregiving families, those not involved with the child welfare system. Since 2000, much of their research examines the protective factors in informal kinship care arrangements (Jane Addams College of Social Work, The Kinship Care Project, 1992).

The National Association of Black Social Workers (NABSW) has for decades tried to dispel the myth that African American families do not adopt or are not available. The NABSW highlights programs throughout the country that are actively involved in finding African American adoptive families. They have engaged in several proactive efforts. For example, there's adoption exchange, which allows for a much larger pool of agencies across states that place African American children with African American families.

The Controversy Behind Group (Home) Care

Contrary to what service providers would like to believe, youth have a lot of agency and control over their own lives—where they are placed, how they are viewed in that placement, and what it takes to be moved to another placement. Ungar (2004) admits, "There is a lot of power which comes from *being placed*" (p. 174). Youth see every new placement as a way to redefine themselves. One key to figuring out whether or not youth will *make it* in a placement (long-term) involves the different meaning they give to one type of placement (e.g., residential) over another (e.g., foster home). Quickly, youth come to know what it takes to *survive inside*.

The move in the late nineteenth century from congregate to cottage-style institutions was an attempt to achieve a more family-like atmosphere (Rothman, 1980). The belief was that all children deserve a family, especially if they are younger than thirteen. The degree to which a placement was viewed as permanent is associated with children's behavior adjustment (Dubowitz et al., 1993). They found that children whose permanency plans were unclear were at greater risk for externalizing behaviors than were children with clear plans. For example, most adolescents in out-of-home care are rarely concerned about feelings of guilt over certain problem behaviors they exhibit because they see these behaviors as natural reactions to their current situation.

Maier (1965) identifies social group work as one solution for healthy development among youth. "Group living constitutes a life experience replacing temporarily dislocated primary family living ... The living group can easily be designated as the market place of ego development" (p. 34). He bases some of this argument on the history and impact of social movements. He also discusses the social worker's goal in addressing social problems in society. Finally, he identifies the significance of group living situations for youth (dependency, coping arena, place of belonging, and reference system). Group work can increase youth's sense of belonging and self-worth, stimulate ideas, and move them toward maturation and coincidently, goal attainment.

Social learning perspectives on adolescent development address the importance of modeling, imitation, and identification. With the onset of adolescence, parents and teachers frequently decline as important models, at least in regard to issues and choices that are of immediate consequences (Muuss, 1975). During adolescence it is the peer group and selected entertainment heroes who become increasingly important as models, especially if communication between parents and adolescents breaks down. The peer group is influential in adolescents' verbal expressions, hairstyles, clothing, food, and music preferences. The feeling of belonging and acceptance can be very important for youth. Youth growing up in the child welfare system are often seeking a place of belonging. They find comfort in other children who have had similar experiences.

Krueger (2007) argues, "The challenge is to form relationships and create opportunities to learn and grow together with youth" (p. 110). The way youth navigate and make meaning (think) of their experiences in out-of-home placement dictates the choices acts they make and how they solve problems on a daily basis. Krueger discusses the importance of focusing on the "what is" of the moment with youth. Understanding what youth say and the context under which they say it makes all the difference when building relationships with them. Teenagers need their thoughts to be validated by adults who have their best interest in mind. Krueger admits this quest can be difficult if the youth and youth worker have not developed a relationship. The way the relationship between worker and youth develops and triumphs in the midst of change is a learning process for youth and helps their overall development. Youth care workers experience disappointments and letdowns just like they do, but how we respond in these moments is what creates character.

Krueger (1995) gives a somewhat similar explanation of the significance of the relationship between youth and youth worker: "Child and youth care is a modern dance in which workers and youth move in and out of sync" (p. 56). Several factors can contribute to being in sync with youth—rhythm, presence, meaning, atmosphere, transition, activities, counseling crisis, and teamwork. During these interactions with youth workers, youth make meaning of the world.

Life after Aging Out

With almost one third of all children in foster care for three years or more (USDHHS, 2005), research must examine the long-term impact of foster family life, contact with birth families, and foster care experiences (i.e., number of placements and service utilization) on children's trajectories. A longitudinal approach allows researchers to examine the relationship between foster care experiences and child outcomes. The focus should be on the meaning of each experience for the child, family, and case worker.

The Administration on Children, Youth and Families (ACYF) recognizes the critical need to prepare youth effectively for both the challenges and the opportunities that lie beyond emancipation. Through the Federal Independent Living Program (ILP), ACYF supports state child welfare agencies in providing services that help youth sixteen and older build the skills needed to achieve self-sufficiency. The ACYF report, based on a review and analysis of ten years of final reports submitted by all states to ACYF, creates a national picture of the youth served during the first decade of ILP (1987–1996). The report describes ILP services provided to youth and highlights trends and service approaches in the areas of educational and vocational training, employment, budgeting, housing, mental health, health care, and youth involvement.

As youth are discharged from care, they face new responsibilities for their own economic independence and general well-being. To prepare for living self-sufficiently, these youth must develop an understanding of and build skills needed to (US Department of Health and Human Services, 1999)

- pursue or complete their education or vocational training;

- obtain and maintain employment (e.g., learn how to prepare a resume, conduct a successful interview, develop on-the-job skills, communicate effectively with supervisors);
- locate and maintain affordable housing (e.g., learn where to look for an apartment and how to complete a lease);
- manage their money and keep a budget;
- cook meals, keep house, and perform other routines for daily living; and
- access health care and community services.

In addition to the necessary concrete skills and supports, youth also need to continue developing their social and interpersonal skills and building their confidence and self-esteem. The purpose of the ACYF study was to review and analyze data collected and reported in ten years of ILP final reports and related materials. The study team reviewed and extracted data from 464 final reports from all fifty states and the District of Columbia. The ILP materials reflected significant data limitations (US Department of Health and Human Services, 1999).

- Nonstandardized reporting formats resulted in reports that varied widely in terms of content, depth, breadth, and methodology.
- There was a lack of consistent definitions of terms, including concepts such as *served, eligible, completed services, needs assessment, counseling,* and *aftercare.*
- There were inconsistencies in data reported across states and within states (across counties or across years).
- There were differences in the time frames used for collecting and presenting data (e.g., data regarding youth eligible for services, outcome data, etc.).

- There was a lack of information regarding the scope, intensity, and duration of different types of services and the number of youth served by each.
- There were difficulties tracking youth to collect outcome data following discharge.

Research Limitations

Despite the limitations and caution in interpretation, the data collected and analyzed can help to create a valuable picture of ILP services and activities and a sense of the trends and changes over time. Data suggest that many of the youth eligible for services over the decade did not receive ILP services. In thirty states that reported such data in 1996, more than one-third (37 percent) of the total youth eligible for services did not receive any services.

The short- and long-term outcomes for youth served under the ILP are areas of great interest and major concern. Outcome data collected by states for the final reporting process is problematic because of inconsistencies in definitions, differing time periods measured, and difficulties tracking youth after they exit from care. Unfortunately, after exiting care, many youth had difficulties completing educational goals, maintaining jobs, achieving financial self-sufficiency, paying for housing expenses, and accessing health care.

States provided a range of services to youth in care in the areas of educational and vocational support, career planning and employment services, housing and home management, budgeting, health care, mental health and well-being support services, and youth involvement. Large increases were noted in postsecondary educational support, purchase of educational and career resources, home maintenance, personal care (e.g., hygiene, nutrition, and fitness), medical care and education, teen parenting classes, substance abuse education, and youth advisory boards and newsletters. States generally moved from concentrating primarily on concrete tangible skills (e.g., vocational training, job search, and money management) to also addressing important intangible skills such as decision making, communication, and conflict resolution (US Department of Health and Human Services, 1999).

Research on the transition for former foster youth is limited and most of the studies on outcomes for these youth face methodological challenges. They tend to be dated. They include brief follow-up periods (i.e., no more than a year after exit from care). They have low response rates, samples that aren't representative, and small sample sizes, and they do not follow youth prior to exit from foster care (Courtney and Heuring, 2005). Few studies include comparison groups to get an idea of how well these youth are transitioning to adulthood in relation to their peers in the foster care population or general population.

Two Studies Focused on the Experiences of Youth Still in Care and Youth That Aged Out

The Northwest Foster Care Alumni Study and the Midwest Evaluation of the Adult Functioning of Former Foster Youth have tracked outcomes for a sample of youth across several domains, either prospectively (following youth in care and as they age out) or retrospectively (examining current outcomes for young adults who were in care at least a few years ago) and comparing these outcomes to other groups of youth, either those who aged out and/or youth in the general population. Both studies indicate that youth who spent time in foster care during their teenage years tended to have difficulty during the transition to adulthood and beyond. The two reports exclude youth with developmental disabilities or severe mental illness that precluded them from participating as well as youth who were incarcerated or in a psychiatric hospital.

47

The Northwest Foster Care Alumni Study

Researchers with the Northwest Foster Care Alumni Study interviewed and reviewed the case files of 479 foster care youth who were in public or private foster care any time from 1988 to 1998 in Oregon or Washington. On average, they interviewed youth who were 24.2 years old with a range of twenty to thirty-three years old. The youth tended to be females (60 percent versus the 48 percent of females in foster care nationally in 2006). They also tended to have entered care as adolescents (11.1 years versus 8.1 years for children entering care in 2006). Nearly 60 percent of the youth in this study were age twelve and older at the time they entered care. And they tended to have exited care between the ages of fifteen and older. (The mean age at exit was 18.5 years old in 2006 for foster youth nationwide.) Young adults experienced these outcomes even though most (83.6 percent) reported having access to *a lot* of child welfare services and support, and about eight of ten (81.5 percent) said that they felt loved while in care. These findings suggest that a number of factors, including the reasons they entered care, family dynamics, and access to services and support before and after aging out of care, have likely influenced how well they function as adults (Pecora et al., 2005).

The study compared the mental health status, educational attainment, and employment and finances for the foster care alumni to those of the general population (Wulczyn et al., 2002). Regarding mental health, more than 54 percent of foster care "alumni" (as referred to in this study) had at least one mental health problem (depression, social phobia, panic disorder, and post-traumatic stress disorder, among others) compared to 22.1 percent of the general population. About one quarter of the alumni experienced post-traumatic stress disorder (PTSD). This figure is greater than the prevalence of PTSD among Vietnam or Iraq war veterans—about 15 percent. Alumni tended to have similar recovery rates as their counterparts in the general population for major depression, panic syndrome, and alcohol dependency, but lower rates of recovery for other disorders such as generalized anxiety disorder, PTSD, social phobia, and bulimia.

Regarding education, while alumni have obtained a high school diploma or passed the general education development (GED) test at the same rates as twenty-five- to thirty-four-year-olds generally (84.5 percent versus 87.3 percent), they are much less likely to have a bachelor's degree (1.8 percent versus 22.5 percent of all young people). In relation to employment and finances, one-third of alumni reported living below the poverty line, which is three times the national poverty rate. Further, almost 17 percent were dependent on Temporary Assistance for Needy Families (TANF) compared to 3 percent of the general population (although the high rate of participation in Oregon and Washington could have been due in part to TANF rules in those states). The alumni employment rate was 80 percent, while the general employment rate was 95 percent. Other indicators show that alumni were not financially secure. One-third lacked health insurance (versus 18 percent of the general population), and 22 percent were homeless at least one day during the year after they left foster care (versus 1 percent of the general population who were homeless within the previous year).

The Midwest Evaluation of the Adult Functioning of Former Foster Youth

Few foster care alumni studies follow youth while in care through the time they leave care and beyond. The Midwest Evaluation is an ongoing study that tracks six hundred or more current and former foster youth in three states—Illinois, Iowa, and Wisconsin. All of the surveyed youth entered care prior to their sixteenth birthday. Surveyed youth responded to researcher questions about outcomes in three data collection waves. At wave 1, they were age seventeen or eighteen, at which time most were in care. At wave 2, they were ages nineteen or twenty, at which time some remained in care. And at wave 3, they were ages twenty or twenty-one and no longer in care. Of those who remained in care beyond age eighteen, all were in Illinois, the only state of the three that retains court jurisdiction of foster youth (with the youth's permission) until age twenty-one. The Midwest Evaluation researchers expect to track youth outcomes at age twenty-three and possibly beyond (Courtney et al., 2005).

At wave 1, from 50 to 70 percent of youth in care reported receiving any one category of independent living services (educational services, employment/vocational support, budget and financial management support, housing services, health education services, and youth development services). At wave 2, not more than half of the youth in care reported receiving at least one independent living service. At wave 3, receipt of services decreased for youth regardless of whether they remained in care. No more than approximately one-third of the youth reported receiving at least one independent living service. For youth in the third wave, about one-third had left foster care within the previous twelve months, and another one-third had left care in the past three to four years. The balance of youth had left care one to three years prior or more than four years prior.

Nearly nine of ten were age twenty-one, and 53.2 percent were female. Most (55.6 percent) identified as African American, followed by white (32.5 percent), multiracial (9.5 percent), and other races. Approximately 8 percent identified as Hispanic. Almost two-thirds of youth (64.3 percent) reported feeling lucky to have been placed in foster care compared with 9.7 percent who neither agreed nor disagreed with feeling lucky and 26 percent who disagreed or strongly disagreed. About the same proportions of youth reported feeling satisfied with their experiences in foster care. Youth were also asked about receipt of independent living services across six domains—education, vocational training or employment, budgeting and financial management, health education, housing, and youth development such as conferences and leadership development activities. For each of the domains, about one-third of the youth or less reported having received relevant services since the wave 2 study, and no more than one-third reported having received relevant services since they were discharged from care. The researchers speculated that the services were available but that the young adults did not perceive a need for the services or were unable to access them.

At ages twenty-one or twenty-two, most youth reported strong family ties, with 94 percent having said that they felt somewhat or very close to at least one biological family member. The greatest share of youth reported feeling very close to their siblings followed by another relative (aunt, uncle, or cousin), grandparent, biological mother, and biological father. The surveyed youth were most likely to be in daily contact (in this order) with their siblings, biological mother, grandparents, and other relatives. Overall, more than half of all youth perceived that some or most of the time, they had social support, such as someone to listen to them (66.1 percent), someone to help with favors (59.2 percent), someone to loan them money (50.3 percent), and some to encourage them to work toward their goals (53.6 percent).

In the Northwest Foster Care Alumni Study of former foster youth ages twenty to thirty-three, about one out of five (22.5 percent) reported being homeless for one day or more within a year of leaving foster care. This figure is slightly higher than the 18 percent of twenty-one-year-olds in the Midwest Evaluation who reported being homeless at least once since exiting care. The housing status of former foster youth is often affected by relationships, education, and employment. Reciprocally, youth who lack housing may have difficulty staying in school and/or maintaining employment (The University of Oklahoma National Child Welfare Resource Center for Youth, 2003).

A study of youth in the Midwest who ran away from foster care between 1993 and 2003 found that the average likelihood of an individual running away from foster care placements increased over this time period. Youth questioned about their runaway experiences cited the following three primary reasons for running from foster care: (1) to reconnect or stay connected to their biological families even if they recognized that their families were neither healthy nor safe; (2) to express their autonomy and find normalcy among sometimes chaotic events; and (3) to maintain surrogate family relationships with nonfamily members. Runaway youth in the study were more likely than their foster care peers to abuse drugs and to have certain mental health disorders (Courtney et al., 2005).

A child is considered missing from foster care if she or he is not in the physical custody of the child welfare agency or the institution or person with whom the child has been placed because of (1) the child's leaving voluntarily without permission (i.e., runaways); (2) the family or nonfamily member's removing the child, either voluntarily or involuntarily, without permission (i.e., abductions); or (3) a lack of oversight by the child welfare agency. The majority of children known to be missing from foster care are runaways. According to the US Department of Health and Human Services, on the last day of 2006, approximately twelve thousand (2 percent) of the 510,000 children in foster care had run away, and another 5,049 had exited the system as runaways (because they were old enough to emancipate and were on runaway status at the age of emancipation).

Most runaways tend to be teenagers (Child Welfare League of America, 1996–2012).

The literature review suggests the long-term effects of out-of-home care are significant. The effects of foster care drift on children (especially length and number of placements) are significant to their development. The constant change in placement makes it difficult for biological families to stay connected (bond, support, provide for) their child in OHC. And this also makes it difficult for youth to attach to other supportive adults they encounter while growing up in OHC. This inability to stay connected to caring adults (e.g., biological parents, previous caregivers, teachers, and friends) is often what hurts them the most in the long run.

With the CPS goal of keeping children safe, research suggests children growing up in out-of-home care actually fare worse than children in the general population in a number of areas because of their inability to stay connected to caring adults. Youth age out of care with no plan, support, place to live, money, and little education. Achieving permanency sooner gives every child a better chance at a healthy development and more positive and long-lasting attachments to caregivers.

My proposed study will explore teenage girls' memories of their experiences before, during, and after their placement in out-of-home care and most importantly, address how they make meaning of their experiences. The goal is for these interviews to create more effective ways of supporting youth growing up in OHC so they become more productive, resourceful, and self-sufficient adults. Only through their stories can we see their struggle and their survival.

National Statistics

- Twenty-five percent of foster youth reported they had been homeless at least one night 2.5 to 4.0 years after exiting foster care.
- Three in ten of the nation's homeless adults report foster care history.
- Fifty-four percent of former foster youth had completed high school.
- Thirty-eight percent of former foster youth maintained employment for one year.
- Sixty percent of young women had children 2.5 to 4.0 years after leaving foster care.

(Child Welfare League of America, 1996–2012)

CHAPTER 3

Methodology

Questions and/or Hypotheses

IN THIS CHAPTER, I OUTLINE THE METHODOLOGICAL details of my study. This study utilizes narrative research methodology and qualitative interviews from former foster youth to explore their experiences before, during, and after their placement in out-of-home care (OHC). This study focuses on how they interpret and make meaning of their experiences. In addition, the research seeks to understand how former foster youth face day-to-day living situations and overcome their challenges. More importantly, what past experiences do they feel have most affected their current situation? The purpose of this study was to describe the lived experiences of young women who aged out of OHC.

The Design: Method and Procedures

Narrative method includes an exploration of biographic experiences or details as narrated by the person who has lived them (Chase, 2005). The narrative can be oral or written. Data gathering occurs naturally, during conversation, an interview, or fieldwork. This data can be a story (referring to a specific event) or one's entire life experiences. "What is distinct about the contemporary narrative approach to research is the focus on meaning making, as opposed to merely documenting a history or an experience" (Rudestam and Newton, 2014, p. 49). For example, how do participants come to understand an experience? What does their story reveal about them and the world (as they know/ see it)? In this study narrative research was used to focus on eight young women who have aged out of OHC, on the data from their stories (before, during, and after OHC), and on the analysis of the experiences for the meanings the individuals make.

"Narrative can be both a method and *the phenomenon* of study," said Pinnegar and Daynes (2006, p. 54). As a method, it begins with the experiences as expressed in lived and told stories of individuals. As a specific type of qualitative design, "narrative is understood as a spoke or written text giving an account of an event/action or series of events/actions, chronologically connected" (Czarniawska, 2004, p. 70). Young women involved in the study were asked to give an account of their lives (significant attachments, separations, placements, activities, obstacles, and accomplishments).

Cortazzi suggests that "the chronology of narrative research, with an emphasis on sequence, sets narrative apart from other genres of research" (1993, p. 74). However, for this particular study, the sequence is less important. More important is where epiphanies are situated in their story. How do they interpret the meaning of their experiences in relation to other events in their lives during that time period? Kermode (1981) referred to the untold stories "narrative secrets." This involves paying as much attention to the stories not told as to those that are. The central idea is obvious when it is understood that people are both "living their stories in an ongoing experiential context and telling their stories in words as they reflect upon life and explain themselves to others" (Connelly and Clandinin, 2013, p. 4). In other words, people are constantly living, telling, retelling, and reliving stories.

There are two approaches to narrative research. The first approach focuses on *analytic strategies*, for example, the "analysis of narratives," which involves creating descriptions of themes across stories and the "narrative analysis," which involves collecting descriptions of events and putting them into a story with a plot. The second approach focuses on the *forms* of narrative research most commonly practiced. For example, an oral history consists of gathering personal reflections of events and their causes and effects from one individual or several individuals (Plummer, 1983). A life history is described as "the narrative of an individual life," which originates reactively rather than spontaneously (Long, 1999). These are first-person accounts shaped by the researcher.

Rationale for Using the Narrative Method

All six qualitative research methods (narrative, phenomenology, grounded theory, ethnography, case study, and interpretive) follow a general process starting with a research problem and question(s) followed by collecting data, analyzing the data, and writing up a report. Many of these methods also use the same data collection processes (i.e., interviews and/or observations). In this section I will give a rationale for using narrative research methodology for this study.

The six most common research methods (previously discussed)

differ in one very important way, specifically what they are each trying to accomplish. For example, exploring a life (narrative research) is different from generating a theory (grounded theory), or describing the behavior of a culture (ethnography). In "narrative research, the inquirer focuses on the stories told by the individual and arranges these stories in chronological order" (Creswell, 2012, p. 102) or according to themes that emerge. In this study, young women share memories surrounding their removal from their biological family and placement in OHC. Young women are asked to discuss significant placements and relationships with caregivers. They are asked to reflect on what experiences made the biggest impact on where they are in life now. Research questions were centered on the participant's description of her feelings, knowledge, and behavior during three periods in her life—family life, growing up in OHC, and aging out.

Initially, when thinking about my research problem and question, my research questions focused more on the essence of being in out-of-home care (OHC) or the essence of being in a particular placement (phenomenology). However, while being in OHC was a very pertinent point in their lives, it became clear there were other very important points (family life) and people who impact how they might have come to understand an experience. A second idea was to conduct a case study to examine a particular placement in order to gain an in-depth understanding of the program and types of activities. Again, this type of study would take the focus away from the girls and be more of an analysis of a particular program (placement). Narrative method is the best method of collecting stories—before, during, and after OHC—or life experiences from these young women. Narrative method keeps the focus on the girls, not the child welfare system or a program/placement.

Qualitative Interviewing

"Qualitative researchers are guests in private spaces of the world. Their manners should be good and their code of ethics strict" (Denzin and Lincoln, 1994, p. 103). The more natural and real the interest by the researcher, the more unique the study. For me, the term *privileged* comes to mind when conducting qualitative research. We are privileged to be allowed *inside* to see or hear what a participant shares—the challenge is that we represent their stories well and honestly just as they tell them. For this study, my focus was answering the question, "What story does each participant have to tell?"

Interviews give us an opportunity to hear the observations of other people. Qualitative interviewing allows us access to places we as researchers may not have been allowed into. Weiss (1994) contends, "We can learn what people perceived and how they interpreted their perceptions. We can learn how events affected their thoughts and feelings" (p. 88). The young women in this study opened the doors to a story that can be told only by them, those who lived and experienced it—the story of the time period before, during, and after their placement in OHC.

Ladson-Billings (1998) contends, "Stories provide the necessary context for understanding, feeling, and interpreting" (p. 49). Frequently, youth in out-of-home care express feeling as if their voice (needs and wants) go unheard and ignored by people *supposedly* advocating for *their* best interest. Within the story there may be epiphanies (where the story line changes dramatically). For foster youth these epiphanies may stem from various memories (e.g., negative memories and positive ones), their first night in OHC, or even memories of an actual placement/caregiver.

The relationship between researcher and participants could create problems during the data collection phase. Weiss and Fine (2000) raise additional questions about "the interviewee's

59

ability to articulate the forces that oppress them, how much of their history may be erased, and what if they chose not to share the difficult aspects of their lives" (Creswell, 2007, p. 140). Sandy (2013) describes microhistorians as one person's story, particularly a person not in a position of power, can speak volumes about a larger phenomenon by illuminating aspects that are typically hidden. In this study my verbal and nonverbal responses must be contained so as not to sway the participants to feel like they cannot tell their story honestly and in its totality (good and bad).

Sampling

"There is no standard size recommended for narrative research, however at least two individuals are necessary for thorough data gathering" (Clandinin and Connelly, 2004; Creswell et al., 2007). I pursued women who meet a purposeful criteria. Eight young women were interviewed, all at least eighteen years old. These young women were first detained after age seven. The young women were placed in OHC after their seventh birthday because the interviews included questions about the memories they have of their biological family life before removal from home. These young women aged out of out-of-home care between one to three years before the interviews and were not be under an existing court order because of the interest in their current daily living situation. I accepted the first eight participants meeting these four criteria who contacted me. Courtney et al. (2010) describe 4 distinct classes of former foster youth in the Midwest Study. They refer to the largest class as the *accelerated adults,* with members of this class being most likely to live on their own and earn a high school diploma. Half have attended college, and they are the most likely to have a college degree too. Nearly two-thirds (63 percent) are female, which is why I am interested in conducting interviews with young women.

Instrumentation

This study conducted qualitative interviews surrounding the lived experiences of young women who had aged out of OHC. What are the similar/different experiences that young women have had? How have these experiences shaped their present outcomes? How has their placement in OHC impacted their ability to attach and maintain meaningful relationships with caregivers, biological parents/siblings, teachers, peers, and coworkers? The goal of the study was to better inform all people working with youth in OHC.

Interview questions were centered on the participant's description of her feelings, knowledge, and behavior at three points in time family life while growing up in OHC and experiencing life after aging out. What were the experiences, stories, turning points, and theories of each participant? Understanding how young girls experienced and faced these times was key to understanding how they now process growing up in OHC.

Rationale for Gathering Data Surrounding Family Life before OHC

I gathered data on family life before OHC in order to explore the importance and the progression toward development (Sears, 1975; Chouinard, 2007; Maier, 1990; Freud, 1923). My protocol included topics such as their relationship with their biological parents and siblings growing up, their fondest memory of their family, and other people who played a significant role in their lives. The protocol questions are grounded in the literature that suggests bonding and attachment are key factors in the healthy development of children (Suttie, 1935; Winnicott, 1956; Loewald, 1978; Mercer, 2006; Mitchell and Ziegler, 2007). Furthermore, the literature indicates that separation has a major effect on children, no matter the age or circumstances (Spitz, 1945; Eyer, 1992; Klaus et al., 1995).

Rationale—Growing Up in Out-of-Home Care

I gathered data on the experiences young women had while growing up in OHC, often bouncing around from one placement to the next (Wulczyn et al., 2002; Maas and Engler, 1959). The literature suggests that a lack of consistency in placement makes it difficult for children in OHC to form bonds/attachments with primary caregivers, youth care workers, teachers, and peers (Courtney et al., 2001; Rosenfeld, Richman, and Bowen, 2000; Berrick, Courtney, and Barth, 1993; Ungar, 2004; Rothman, 1980; Maier, 1965; Muuss, 1975; Krueger, 2007; Krueger, 1995). My protocol included topics such as their initial reactions to being placed in OHC, significant placements and caregivers (good and bad), their relationships with other kids in OHC, their relationship with social workers, placement changes, and their ability to remain connected when placements changed. The protocol questions are grounded in the literature, which suggests what children and their parents know about factors contributing to placement in OHC has a huge effect on their understanding of when and what it takes to return home (Doyle, 1990; Rockhill, 2010; Belsky and Vondra, 1989).

Rationale—Aging Out

I gathered data on the sudden transition from foster care to independent living (Sim, Emerson, O'Brien, Pecora, and Silva, 2008). My protocol included topics such as how youth were prepared for discharge, who helped prepare them, living arrangements after discharge, and the skills and resources they gained while in OHC (education, employment, budgeting). The protocol questions are grounded in the literature, which suggests that adolescents who pass through the child welfare system fare worse than youth in the general population (National Research Council, 1993). The number of foster youth proceeding to post-secondary education is low (Snyder and Tan, 2006). Adolescents who have received child welfare services exhibit more delinquency and fewer social skills than the general population (Wall, Barth, and The NSCAW Research Group, 2005).

Data Collection

Eight participants were interviewed about three points in their life—family life, growing up in OHC, and life after aging out. All eight participants gave verbal and written consent to have their interview audiotaped. I conducted 1 interview with each participant. The interviews were approximately one to two hours in duration. Each participant was paid $25.00 (cash) after each interview. Pseudonyms were used to protect the participants' confidentiality. The interviews took place at the Milwaukee Public Library (Washington Park, Center, Atkinson), the location closest and most convenient for the participant. The interview took place in a small conference room with just me and the participant. Flyers were posted at agencies that work with youth who have aged out of OHC (i.e., Ladelake, Kids Matter, and SDC). Participants were chosen if they met all the criteria. There were four criteria in order to participate in the study. There person needed be a female, not under an existing court order/aged out, have lived in at least one foster and group home, and should have been first removed at or after age seven and aged out for at least one year.

Psychological stress was a potential risk in discussing their lived experiences. Participation in this study was entirely voluntary. Those who decided to take part could have changed their minds and withdrew from the study. Participants were free to withdraw at any time. No participants withdrew from the study. Also, I kept a reference guide of community agencies and offered resources. The data transcribed and collected for the study is stored in a locked cabinet. The tapes will be destroyed at the end of the study.

Icebreakers were used to develop a rapport. Probes were used during the interviews to follow up, elaborate, and clarify responses. Emerson explains, "Even ethnographers who usually write open jottings may at other times make jottings privately, out of sight of those studied ... waiting until just after a scene, incident, or conversation has occurred" (Emerson, 1995, p. 24). I also took notes during the interview and transcribed the audiotapes immediately. Of interest is the way these young women have come to interpret and make meaning of some of the epiphanies in their lives before, during, and after OHC. Who and what is affiliated with their memories of significant placement(s), caregivers, and moments with biological family members?

Data Analysis

Interview Transcriptions and Memos

Eight participants were interviewed. The interviews were approximately one to two hours, and the transcriptions ranged from fifteen to twenty-five pages. The interviews were transcribed by me. I wrote field notes after each interview describing my emotional reactions, the participant's emotional reactions to certain questions, and also knowledge, feelings, and behaviors that were similar across participants. I reread the interview transcriptions, looked over my field notes, and listened to the audiotapes several times to get a better understanding of the feelings, knowledge, behaviors, and emotional tone of the participants.

Developing some manageable classification or coding scheme was my first step of analysis. Without classification there is chaos and confusion. This process involves identifying, coding, categorizing, and labeling the patterns in the data. This process also involves analyzing the core content of the interviews to determine what's significant (Patton, 2002). I introduce themes through the experiences of the participants during three points in life—family life, growing up in OHC, and life after aging out. Here is the process I underwent in categorizing the themes.

Coding Procedures and Themes

Categorization was my second step of analysis. Clandinin and Connelly (2000) refer to writing research texts using an approach to themes in which the researcher looks for common threads or elements across participants. The data collected from the interviews was analyzed according to the themes that emerged. As themes began to emerge, I started sorting—labeling categories, deciding what should be included and excluded, and revising categories. Themes were adjusted until all the data fit in a category. I started with an initial read of the transcripts to understand the general story. I reread the transcripts more than five times to determine the initial codes. Then after further rereading the transcripts and reflecting on the literature review, more specific themes surfaced. The themes within each interview were organized in three stages—preplacement, placement, and postplacement. Themes are also compared and contrasted across participant.

Van Manen (1990) placed emphasis on gaining an understanding of themes by asking, "What is this example an example of?" (p. 86). The themes should have certain qualities such as focus, a simplification of ideas, and a description of the structure of the lived experience. My process involved looking for statements/phrases in the interview transcriptions and examining every single sentence. I looked for common patterns and themes across participants.

Three-Dimensional Space Approach Model

Clandinin and Connelly (2000) best describe my approach to analysis, which is a three-dimensional narrative inquiry space approach—the personal and social (the interaction); the past, present, and future (continuity); and the place (situation). This approach suggests that to understand people, we need to examine not only their personal experiences but also their interactions with other people. For this study it was important to understand not only each girl's knowledge, feelings, and behaviors (during family life, growing up in OHC, and life after aging out) but also their significant interactions with family members, caregivers, other kids in OHC, educators, and other service providers.

The first dimension to this approach is interaction—the personal (conditions, feelings, hopes) and the social (other people's intentions, assumptions, points of view). My participants expressed their hopes and feelings (i.e., reunify with biological family, leave the system, become independent) at different periods of time and discussed how others (i.e., family members, social workers, teachers, and other kids in OHC) responded to these feelings. (Some responses were good, and some responses were not.)

The second dimension to this approach is continuity (the past, present, and future). The participants looked back at their family life to share their feelings, knowledge, and behavior during that time period. They discussed their parents' absence and significant relationships with siblings. The participants looked at their feelings, knowledge, and behavior while growing up in OHC and maneuvering through the system. They discussed significant placements, caregivers, activities, and relationships with peers while in OHC. They discussed a lack of knowledge about the system and age (being young) to justify some of their feelings and behavior while in OHC. They discussed the frustration of changing placements and changing school. The participants looked at their life after aging out (i.e., own apartment, good mother, employed) and discussed ways being in the system may or may not have contributed to their current situation. The participants also discussed regrets and things they should/could have done differently, resulting in a message for current kids in OHC to "never give up."

The third dimension in this approach is situation/place, which involves the context, time, place, and characters. The participants were asked about their feelings, knowledge, and behavior during three points in life—family life, growing up in OHC, and life after aging out. During these interviews the participants shared the circumstances and some background as to why certain things happened (i.e., why they were removed from the home, why placements changed when in OHC, and why they did/did not receive things previously promised to them when they aged out). The participants were specific in time (using their age to connect their knowledge), in place (using placements to connect their frustrations and behaviors), and in characters (using family members, caregivers, other kids in OHC, educators, and social workers to connect specific details about experiences throughout their life).

The researcher needs to have a clear picture of the individual's life. Creswell (2007) explains, "Active collaboration with the participant is necessary, and researchers need to discuss the participant's stories as well as be reflective about their own personal and political background, which shapes how they 'restory' the account" (p. 21). Active collaboration involves the researcher moving from a more formal way of asking questions to a more informal and open conversation. Researchers must collaborate with participants by actively involving them in the research (Clandinin and Connelly, 2000).

Wallen and Fraenkel (2001) explain, "The results of a qualitative study are most effectively presented by means of a narrative, rich in detail also referred to as rich (or thick) *description*" (p. 234). During my study, participants were asked to expand on various stories. The participants were asked to theorize about their lives. Denzin (1989) contends, "Thick description sets up and makes possible interpretation ... and provides the skeletal frame for analysis that leads into interpretation" (p. 101). By this, he means the narrative should present detail, context, and emotion, stimulating self-feelings that ensure the voices, feelings, actions, and meanings of participants are heard. Doing so leads to a study that highlights the individual's life, different theories that relate to experiences they she has had, and unique or general features of her life.

Limitations and Delimitations

Metz (1972, 1980) argues there are two categories of memories. In the first category, memory represents a recollection of past events, a *selective* memory, drawing from one's own perspective. In the second category, memory interrupts fixed narratives with a powerful acknowledgment of human suffering—that is *dangerous memories*. Dangerous memories can be challenging, critical, and hopeful. Psychological stress was a potential risk in discussing their lived experiences. Teens may be *selective* in the way they talk about dangerous memories (e.g., most stories may depict them always doing the right thing or playing on the role of the victim).

According to Giroux (1997), a dangerous memory has two dimensions, "that of hope and that of suffering" (p. 105). Welch

(1985) contends that "we need such memories if we are to find and sustain the strength, resiliency, courage, and hope required for resisting the forces of evil. On the other hand, qualitative research involves the danger of the 'Hollywood plot': the plot in which everything works out well in the end ... Such plots may be ones in which there is thorough and unbending censure ... or they may be ones in which the good intentions of researchers and participants are found in every aspect of the study" (Clandinin and Connelly, 2000). Through these stories we understand how these young women faced day-to-day challenges before, during, and after OHC and in what ways they either remain at risk or have been able to overcome their challenges.

Trauma-Informed Research

A major concern when conducting research with vulnerable populations is the fear of retraumatization. Because the skills and background of researchers differ, it is important to understand ways the researcher can reduce the possibility of retraumatization. Hopper and others (2010) described trauma-informed care for individuals as an orientation toward an understanding of trauma to improve the sensitivity of providers and subsequent service delivery. In conducting research, it is important to assume that participants have been exposed to different variations of trauma, and each participant has coped differently. Recruitment is best if a trusting relationship is established. A safe location should be used to gather data, nd ground rules should be explicit, especially regarding the participants' freedom to stop at any time if the questions become too difficult to answer.

Beverley suggests that "qualitative research depends on its ability to raise consciousness, and thus provoke action to remedy problems of oppressed people" (Beverley, 2000, p. 560). We need to understand more about the experiences of these young women in hopes of stopping the circumstances that cause their reoccurrence. My study hopes to contribute to our understanding by learning from the perspective of privileged knowers—former foster youth who grew up in OHC.

Validation

After completing a study, qualitative researchers ask one very important question, "Did I get it right?" (Stake, 1995, p. 62). Researchers look to themselves, the participants, and the readers for answers to this very important question. There are several perspectives on the importance of validation in qualitative research. For example, Lincoln and Guba (1985) feel validation is necessary but have used alternative terms such as trustworthiness of the study, credibility, authenticity, transferability, and dependability. Eisner (1991) refers to the term *credibility* instead of validation. He contends that we seek a union of evidence that creates confidence about our observations, conclusions, and interpretations. Wolcott (1990) had little use for validation, suggesting that "validation does not guide nor inform" (p. 144). His goal was to identify (and understand) critical elements and draw interpretations from them not to convince anyone of anything. Finally, Angen (2000) suggested that validation is "a judgment of the trustworthiness or goodness of a piece of research" (p. 112).

Creswell (2007, p. 214) describes a *good* narrative study as one that

- "focuses on a single individual (or two or three individuals),
- collects stories about a significant issue related to this individuals life,

- develops a chronology that connects different phases or aspects of a story,
- tells a story that restories the story of the participants in the study,
- tells a persuasive story told in a literary way, [and]
- reports themes that build from the story to tell a broader analysis

For my study, several of these criteria were taken into account. For example, my study focused on eight young women who all aged out of OHC for at least one year before the interview and who were first detained after age seven. My data collection consisted of in-depth interviews regarding their experiences before, during, and after OHC. I connected different phases and aspects of their story. My goal was to authentically recall the story the participants were telling. My data analysis included themes that emerge from their stories, and a discussion of me (as the researcher) will be included as well.

My study utilized one validation strategies. Rich, thick description enables the reader to transfer information to other settings and to determine whether findings can be transferred "because of shared experiences" (Erlandson et al., 1993, p. 45). In this study the participants were asked to elaborate, explain, and describe stories with as much detail as possible.

Some limitations to conducting interviews with this group of teenage girls resonate with all studies involving adolescents—honesty in disclosure. Are the participants being truthful or going for a *shock factor*? A second limitation to conducting interviews involves (possibly) the researcher's inability to control nonverbal responses regarding some of the experiences shared about the female's life history. Although the results may not be generalizable to the larger population, I was curious to know whether somewhat similar emotions, struggles, frustrations, obstacles, triumphs, and milestones were expressed by the participants, emerging in the themes that came after coding my data.

Reliability

Reliability can be addressed in qualitative research if the researcher obtains detailed field notes by using a good-quality tape recorder and by transcribing the tape (Silverman, 2005). In my study, participants' interviews were tape-recorded (with their permission), and the tapes were transcribed to indicate crucial pauses or overlaps. The interviews were transcribed by me. I coded the data once the interviews had been transcribed.

Reliability addresses the question of whether similar data collection methods can be used with other populations or participants. For example, other studies could include teen moms growing up in OHC and boys growing up in OHC. The narrative research methodology and qualitative interviews could be used for a study involving either of the two populations. A longitudinal (generational) study involving women who grew up in OHC who are now case heads (with children of their own growing up in OHC) would be very insightful as well.

Researcher Positionality Statement

In narrative research, a key theme has been the turn toward the relationship between the researcher and the researched in which both parties learn and change in the encounter (Pinnegar and Daynes, 2006). What led me to this area of research is a state-licensed group foster home that I own called Home 4 the Heart, Inc. Home 4 the Heart is a group home for teenage girls ages twelve to seventeen, specialized for youth with independent living needs. Over the past nine years, I have worked with more than eighty girls in this small, five-bed group home (which I also called *my family home* for more than thirty years), each girl with a different family history and different obstacles, goals, and outcomes. In this position, it has taken a great deal of creativity on my part to support, assist, and advocate for my girls at Home 4 the Heart.

My reactions after the interviews ranged from overwhelming sadness over the feelings of loss, hopelessness, and pain they experienced ... to frustration over the lack of knowledge, support, and resources they had ... to hope, optimism, and faith that clear things could be done differently to help make life somewhat better for kids in OHC, starting with me and *my girls* at Home 4 the Heart. I have enormous empathy for girls who are growing up in OHC, and I also have an interest in their overall well-being. Most importantly, I have learned the significance of giving them a voice and helping them learn the most beneficial ways of getting their voice heard by all the people they encounter.

The hope is that these detailed interviews will give a glimpse into the journey that these young women have faced. The purpose of this study was to show how young women who grew up in OHC have learned to live independently. What helped or hindered this process? More importantly, what day-to-day experiences do they feel most affected their outcome? The researcher and the researched learn and change throughout the interview process. In the process, the parties negotiate the meaning of the stories, adding a validation check to the analysis (Creswell and Miller, 2000).

Summary

In this chapter I gave a detailed justification of the methodology of choice and data gathering techniques. Narrative methodology gets at the heart of the lived experiences these young women in OHC have had to face. How do they see/feel that these experiences impacted their life now? The purpose of this study was to share the experiences that former foster youth have in OHC so that we may create services to better prepare them to live independently after leaving OHC.

CHAPTER 4

Data Analysis

Overview of the Study

THIS STUDY EXAMINED THE FEELINGS, KNOWLEDGE, and behavior of former foster youth at three points in life—family life (preplacement), growing up in OHC (placement), and after aging out (postplacement). Narrative methodology was the research method used in order to not only document their experiences but also how they make meaning of the experiences.

The eight narratives tell each participant's story. The participants discussed their lives preplacement (e.g., their bonds with biological parents and siblings, their fondest memory with their family, and other people who played a significant role in their lives). The participants discussed their lives while in OHC, significant placements, and caregivers. The participants shared their feelings and behavior when placements changed, which was frequently. They shared their frustrations with social workers, teachers, and especially extended family members (for not saving them from OHC). Finally, the participants talked about their lives now postplacement. The participants gave credit to those who helped prepare them to age out and shared some of the skills and resources they gained while in OHC. Participants opened up about personal regrets and the things they missed the most and least after being discharged from OHC. Participants ended the interview with a message for other kids in OHC, parents and other caregivers, social workers, and even teachers. The themes from each participant's interview were then compared with the other participants. A discussion of what was similar and different across interviews is also in this chapter.

Narratives
Interview #1—"Gee Gee"

Gee Gee and I spoke on the phone and scheduled a time to meet at Washington Park Library. As I walked to the library entrance, there she stood—short, brown skin, and with a huge smile. I appreciated that smile because I was already so nervous about her comfort level with the interview questions.

We were placed in a larger room, big enough for eight to ten people, so before starting the interview, I had to rearrange the furniture a little just so the tape recorder could adequately pick up the sound of both our voices.

Gee Gee started the interview with a smile as she introduced herself and told me that she was a new mother. Then she burst out into laughter, and both of us seemed more at ease.

Preplacement

No Ties, No Tree, No Choice

During the interview, Gee Gee and I talked about her family experiences before she was placed in out of home care. She explained that her mom had passed away before she was placed in out-of-home care. The memory of her mom's passing caused her to cry during the interview. While talking about her family background, she mentioned a strong connection to her mother, even regularly visiting her grave site on Mother's Day. Gee Gee didn't appear to have a relationship with her father or knowledge of where her father lived. Her comments about him were less emotional.

Gee Gee also talked about her grandmother and her siblings. Gee Gee's and her grandmother's relationship seemed pivotal, particularly in the months immediately following her mother's passing. She spoke of her grandmother fondly.

My granny, until she passed. I was close to her. I stayed with her two to three months after mom passed. I just remember my granny.

Gee Gee also has siblings that she remembered being really close to as a child. She was the oldest and her younger siblings found comfort in having her as a sibling.

So he always wanted to sleep with me, and she always wanted to follow after me so much (laughing). My brother, he was scared of the dark. My sister is going to speak her mind and tell you how she feels. Me? I'm basically like that! That's where she gets it from.

She bursts out laughing. I can tell she enjoyed remembering those times with her siblings. These memories took her back to a happy place. She remembered what they meant and still mean to her and what she meant to them.

However, she went on to clarify:

But it's certain types of stuff I will be quiet up on. Like, I know the time to speak.

During the rest of our conversation, I got the impression that this clarification was important for her to say and for me to know. I think it came from a place of growth and lessons learned. For example, Gee Gee shared that because of "the system," her and her siblings were split up. She was frustrated that her and her siblings lost all contact because of the placement strategy. Moreover, she was frustrated that she had no choice in whether she could have relationships with her siblings, and she was frustrated that she was adopted without her input or permission. As she spoke about her placement, she was even more frustrated that her identity was taken, which would ultimately impact the ability of her and her siblings to connect.

And my brother and sister been in the system as long as I been in the system and I don't know where they at. We all got split up, but I remember a little about them. They ain't gonna know me as "X" My real name is "Y" my adopted name is "X". The people I got adopted by wanted me to have that name ("X"), we went to court, and that was it. I ain't have no choice really.

She used her hands to draw the connection as to how one thing led to another thing and ultimately resulted in her and her siblings losing all contact. She mentioned that even with the help of social media, her and her siblings may never find their way back to one another.

Toward the end of our conversation about her preplacement experiences, she revealed that the passing of her mother, the death of grandmother, and the forced separation from her siblings led her to change and create emotional distances between her and others.

I wasn't really close to nobody. I always had that mind frame where I didn't care about nothing. 'Cause my mom passed. It's like I didn't have nobody so I was always like I just don't care about nothing. Like what's there to care about?

She started to tear up, and I ask her if she needed a minute, but she said she was okay.

Placement

Lies, Dreams, and Memories

Gee Gee had childhood memories of her mother and her mother's passing, but one of her foster mothers was not up front about her mother being deceased. Instead her foster mother implied that her birth mother was choosing not to pick her up. Gee Gee pursued the truth by asking questions as she got older, and the foster mother relented and confirmed.

What they was telling me as to why I was in the system? I heard all kinds of lies. Like the lady that was my foster mama, she didn't want to tell me. I was curious but it was lies ... like she (my biological mom) is around but she don't come and get you all types of stuff. But when I started getting older, I started asking questions. Where my mama at? And they like ... She passed.

Gee Gee also shared another lie—the lie of *family* when she was adopted by an unscrupulous person. During Gee Gee's adoption process, she had mixed feelings. There were times she was happy and wanted to be adopted, but others when she was unsure of her adopted mother's true intentions. Unfortunately, it was not until her adoption was finalized and her social worker stopped coming by to check on her, she came to understand her foster mom's true feelings toward her.

Like you know when social workers come into the house to check up on you … you be like yea they nice (they act nice to you). Like okay. They will ask me how is she treating you. And I would be like good. I wanna stay! I wanna stay! Then they start talking about adoption and all this extra stuff. Things started to change. Like (my adopted mom would say) I don't need them white people in my business. By the time I got adopted, the social worker stopped coming! They stopped checking up on me. So she (adopted mom) feel like now she can do whatever. So she started beating me, locking me in my room, sending me to school with black eyes, and she pushed me out of a moving car.

This was difficult for Gee Gee to talk about and even believe. She went on to say that she forgave her but would never forget this incident. These experiences also made her more protective of her own child. She refused to even allow this woman to her see her child.

On the other hand, Gee Gee had positive memories and experiences of *family* during a group home placement. She explained that being "taught right from wrong" was actually seen as showing genuine care, even though at the time, she may not have wanted to hear it because she just wanted to do what she wanted to do.

I like that group home because it's like they care. It's like family. They take you in. They show you right from wrong,

and if you don't like it, they still be there instead of giving up on you. That made me change my ways. I became so close to them. As far as the kids, I looked at them as my little sisters because they were all younger than me.

When asked what she missed most, she screamed, "The allowance!" She went on to say that she missed going to fun places and going out to eat. She acknowledged that she was not always excited to go with the girls on outings. Sometimes she wanted to be a rebel because she felt it was just more fun! She described herself as a tomboy who smoked black and mild cigars, and she would like to hang out and kick it on the block—that is, until the day her group home director surprised her, put her in the car, and took her back to the group home. She laughed and admitted that hanging out was not so much fun anymore after that. So it should be no surprise that when asked what she missed the least about out of home care, she laughed hysterically and said, "Curfew!" She went on to say she was expected to be in by 8:00 p.m. and that was when the fun was just getting started.

Gee Gee shared how the placements and replacements impacted her a great deal emotionally.

After the third foster home, yea, I cried because I liked them, and I started getting used to it. But then after I just moved so much, I just was like ... oh, time to go! I already know! I don't care! I was on medication, and I had a problem, as far as a mental problem ADHD. I was messed up in the head, like from what I had saw. They was like she is just too much! I can't deal with her. She don't wanna take her medication.

Just like some placements, Gee Gee's memory of school was not all good. Although she denied having to change schools when she changed placements, she did mention the stigmatism that was attached to her when students and teachers discovered she was a foster kid. Once this information was discovered, she recalls inappropriate comments made by teachers, jokes from the kids, and many questions she simply did not know how to answer. The questions from school led to frustration, which led to fights. One fight happened a week before graduation, resulting in Gee Gee not receiving her high school diploma.

I got talked about a lot growing up in school. As far as one time a teacher told me (while I was laughing), the teacher walked out of the classroom, and when he came back, he like Ms ????? I don't know why you're laughing ... You need to find your real mama! And I just snapped off! Because they started seeing different women coming into the classroom and they know they not my mom. So they start looking like why she got five to ten different moms? Then the teachers and students start saying, "Oh, you in foster care?" Then they start asking questions. The kids used to pick on me and say you aint got no real mama. I used to get in a lot of fights.

Gee Gee knows how important her education is and does express wanting to eventually get her high school diploma. This was a perfect transition into our postplacement conversation.

Postplacement

Don't Sabotage Yourself

Gee Gee recalled being offered several job opportunities but never having a job. She agrees that she was given the chance and the opportunity, but she would just sabotage herself. She laughed as she remembered the frustration she felt during job interviews. She was so excited to get the call about the interview;

however, she admitted to feeling irritated by all the interview questions. And she shared these frustrations during the interview. She would sigh loudly and tell the person he or she was asking too many questions.

She knew this lack of employment did not help her housing options after aging out. She was given the opportunity to have her own apartment if she changed her behavior, but she admitted that she never did. As a result, she was denied free housing through a program for independent living. If it was not for her group home director, she would have been left with a sheet of bus tickets and a list of shelters.

She (group home owner) started to tell me how to set up doctor's appointments on my own, how to go down to the buildings to do stuff on my own, and how to move my mail to other places. She helped me budget and save. She helped me get an account and everything. She helped me grow. She gave me my first house. They wouldn't give me a house at all. They just wanted to give me a list of shelters and bus tickets and send me on my way. I'm not gonna lose this house! And I still have my house ever since I got out of the system.

Leaving home care with the death of her mother and the separation from her siblings as a constant emotional burden caused Gee Gee to look at life differently now. She felt like she had no biological relatives that she could call on and be excited to spend time with. Other than the relationships she had with previous caregivers and other girls from out of home care, she had no one she felt she could depend on in times of need because even those relationships had changed (and become more distant). She found it difficult to delight in holidays because those were the times she missed having biological family the most.

I don't have a real family. As far as me, I can't say I'm about to go over my sister's house. I'm about to go have fun with my sister. Like I don't have no family that's going to be really there for me. My mama's gone. I don't celebrate no holidays—holidays that have to do with mom, dad, and family ... don't celebrate no holidays! I celebrate now because I have a daughter, and I don't want her to grow up how I grew up. But before I had my daughter, I didn't celebrate no holidays.

Even though Gee Gee had strong negative feelings toward holidays and family celebrations. She still offered optimism and encouragement as a message to other kid in similar situations.

To the kids ... do right and go to school! Be a kid! You don't have to worry about bills. You can just get dressed and go to school and live yo life because when you get out her on your own, it's hard!

For the parents ... cherish your kids because when they're gone, you ain't got them no more. And they gonna look at you like ... they're going to hate you for the rest of your life. They ain't gonna hate you, but they gonna know what you did to them, and they're gonna feel some type of way.

Gee Gee concluded that she loved her dad and would still love to see him again one day!

Interview #2—"Tee Tee"

Tee Tee and I spoke on the phone and agreed to meet at Central Library downtown. The first thing I noticed was her strong African accent.

We met in a small room near the front entrance of the

library. I immediately noticed that she did not appear to be excited about participating in this interview. I introduced myself and shook her hand, but she barely cracked a smile.

Preplacement

Death and Disarray

Tee Tee made it clear from the beginning of the interview that she knew of her mom and dad but she never lived with them and had no bond with either of them. Her father was around until she was four years old. Then he had another child, and that baby became his responsibility. So he disappeared from Tee Tee's life. Her mother was nineteen when she gave birth to Tee Tee; however, she wasn't ready to take on the role of a mother. Instead she just ran the streets. Her mother was incarcerated because she tried to kill a man who was raping her.

To be honest, I didn't feel close to neither. Because my father, I knew of him, but like there's no bond like I know who this person is. And where as my mother, my last memory of her I was sixteen, but like before that. It was the same as my father. I knew of her, but there was no steady relationship. I was always like yea, I know of you, but I'm not going to bond with the relationship, like it's not there.

Tee Tee's grandmother took guardianship of her after her mom went to jail. Tee Tee was raised by her grandmother along with her five aunts to the point where they all felt like siblings growing up together. Other than her grandmother, Tee Tee was close to one of her aunts, who ended up having a baby girl that she was also very close to. She remained close to this aunt up until the day she died of cancer, and she vowed to watch out for her cousin, who was six years younger.

Tee Tee remembered life being good, and she was happy living with her grandmother until the death of her second aunt. She explained how the death of her second aunt had a huge impact on her grandmother. Her grandmother was closest to this daughter. This aunt died tragically in a house fire in Milwaukee, while her grandma was living in Las Vegas and raising Tee Tee and her cousin. Tee Tee said her grandmother was a paranoid schizophrenic who broke down after her second daughter's death, and just couldn't take care of her (or her cousin) anymore.

Tee Tee did not acknowledge any special relationships with her (half) sibling; however, she spoke very highly of her younger cousin. Tee Tee talked about being close to this cousin since she was first born, and even more so after her mother passed away from cancer. Tee Tee felt responsible for this cousin ever since her aunt died and even more after being placed in out-of-home care.

Placement

Trial and Terror

Tee Tee mentioned feeling so confused when first placed in out-of-home care.

I was just in shock more than anything because I don't know anything about this situation (being in out-of-home care). It was confusing, and I was still young. So it was like I was hurt, but I wasn't mad at her (grandmother). You know I understood.

She just wanted to be placed somewhere and be stable.

Unfortunately, this rarely happened. Tee Tee admitted that finding placements that would take both of them was difficult. Caregivers would not want her because she was too old, while her cousin was still young. However, she was adamant about not separating from her cousin. She felt like they should keep moving around until they found someone who was willing to take both of them.

When eventually placed, she describes a lot of caregivers as being "in it for the money."

Other group homes and foster homes, the only thing they really cared about was ... umm, okay, I didn't get paid while you were gone!

She remembered one caregiver used the funds (for their care) to get her house repaired. Tee Tee sadly remembered going into placements with just the clothes on her back and one suitcase and leaving the same way. She remembers being molested and both physically and mentally abused in a foster home placement.

Surprising to her, she saw group homes as the best placement options for her. She identified a certain pressure that comes along with a traditional foster home placement—the pressure of someone trying to replace your parent. Instead group homes offered structure and a set schedule, and no one was there trying to be your parent.

When asked how changing placements impacted Tee Tee. Tee Tee referred to herself as a *terror*. She swept in and out of foster homes and group homes like a *tornado* because she didn't know how to express herself in words. She laughed as she remembered going from respite to detention and then to an out-of-county placement in Eau Claire because of her out-of-control behaviors.

It was confusing, and I was still young. I didn't listen. I was just a wild child, period. I didn't want to hear, this is what you're doing wrong and should try something different. I was trying to be a teenager because I felt like it was taken away from me. I felt like I didn't get my freedom, so I'm gonna do it now. I feel like they didn't listen, they felt like they knew what was best.

Tee Tee recalled having "crisis workers" and several team meetings (some of which she didn't attend). But it wasn't until she met a mentor who would understand her and help her make sense of the situation she was in. This lady was able to shed light on the situation, and Tee Tee felt comfortable sharing her inner struggles with her.

Tee Tee had one attempt at reunification with her aunt. Unfortunately, she never got along with this particular aunt. According to her, this aunt was the youngest of her grandmother's daughters, and they were raised so close together that there was a lot of competition. She also harbored resentment toward this aunt for not sharing her grandmother's breast cancer diagnosis. By the time Tee Tee found out her grandmother was battling cancer, her guardian was already dead. Tee Tee thought of all the conversations she'd had with her aunt. She would ask about her grandmother, but she never got an answer as to where she was and how she was doing.

Tee Tee said shortly after she and her cousin moved in with her aunt, this particular aunt began showing favoritism. She tried to talk to her aunt several times, but they never got to the root of the problem. Tee Tee endured abuse for as long as she could before running away and leaving her aunt's home. She refused to return after school one day because she lost her aunt's house keys. Her aunt had already warned her about the keys, so she was afraid to go back to her aunt's house and face more abuse. So she returned to out-of-home care. Her aunt used that decision against her and created a huge wedge between her and her cousin. Her aunt made it seem like Tee Tee had turned her back on her younger cousin when that wasn't the case at all.

Tee Tee ended up quickly resenting this decision once she started to reexperience the roller-coaster ride of different placements.

When it first happened, I was nervous, but when it got so frequent, I'd have to change my address at school, meet new staff (caregivers), I was like, this is getting old. So I felt like I gave up. I feel like I should have changed my attitude and adjusted to the different people in the different places.

Tee Tee's school did not change when her placements changed; however, she did admit that her attitude at school and toward school changed when her placements changed (which was frequently). She felt other kids were in the same situation (foster care), but hers was being broadcasted throughout the school. She was smart, but she ended up with an IEP because her attendance was so poor; on top of that, she did things to get kicked out of school when she did attend. She felt like a smaller school would have been a much better fit. She was absent from school for good reasons, including moving to another placement, but this still hurt her a great deal academically. She was chronically truant. She received truancy letters but still never went to school and ultimately did not graduate.

Postplacement

If I Knew Then What I Know Now

As Tee Tee reflected on her time in the system and more importantly, how she felt about her current circumstances, she said she regretted taking things for granted.

Don't take anything you love or long for, for granted. I messed up a lot of opportunities to do stuff and see things just from being angry. I went into a phase where I didn't care. I gave up. I didn't care anything. I felt like I was the only person on the face of this earth. I shut myself out from everyone when I found out my grandmother died and my aunt took away my cousin.

On the other hand, Tee Tee acknowledged having more than ten jobs. She had always worked and even volunteered with younger children. She let her guard down with her social worker (who she initially felt had it out for her after sending her to Eau Claire). Both her social worker and mom helped her prepare for discharge. She felt the most important lesson she learned was how to act in different situations. Although she missed some of her old roommates, she did not miss the times when she didn't get her way.

You guys (social workers) are here to help us, but when you ask us our opinion on something, I feel like they didn't listen. They felt like they knew what was best.

Tee Tee's message is simple.

To biological parents, never threaten to give your kids to the system or put your kids in the system. There is a big difference between kids who grow up in out-of-home care and those that do not. Without going into detail, she claimed the struggles and things kids in out-of-home care deal with were different than other kids. She did not want any kid to have to go through this.

Don't tell them that you will give them to the state! This is my biggest pet peeve. Kids that grew up in the system, it took a toll on all of us. So if you care, you wouldn't let your child go in the system.

Her message for teenagers is stay on the right path and don't mess up your chance of getting your life together. She felt she missed out because of "stupid things" like boys, fighting, and AWOLing.

Interview #3—"Fee Fee"

Fee Fee and I agreed to meet at Central Library. We were given a small conference room upstairs. Upon meeting Fee Fee, the first thing I noticed was her saggy jeans and baseball hat to the back. She was short and round. As soon as she sat down, she slouched back in the seat and motioned me to start the interview. The first thing I noticed was her voice and how the dialect she used did not match her outward appearance. She was very well spoken.

Preplacement

Learning How to Make It Happen

Fee Fee described her life before out-of-home care as not being so great. She grew up in what she refers to as "poverty and the projects." She remembered not having food in the house to eat. She described her mom as cool, sweet, and always on the go until she got sick.

Fee Fee talked about her mom's illnesses and how it took a toll on the family. Her mom's health was failing. She was diabetic and partially blind in one eye. She suffered from hypertension and scoliosis. Fee Fee also had a younger brother and a younger sister who lived with her mom.

Fee Fee described her dad as being in and out. He was on drugs and sick too. Fee Fee had one older brother who lived with her dad, but he was killed. Fee Fee would stay with her dad when she and her mom were arguing. She felt there were times when her mom did not understand the type of life she lived.

Fee Fee felt that in many ways she was just like her mom. She was strong. She was the oldest and wanted to make sure her younger siblings were okay. But she could not understand why her mom did not understand her way of thinking.

Any mother who raised their child should know the same capabilities they had in them were instilled in their child. When I saw my mom couldn't get out of bed, then it was on me as the oldest to make it happen.

She remembered getting tissue and cigarettes for her mom. She knew her mom did not want her to know how sick she was, but she could see for herself that her health was failing. Fee Fee described her relationship with her siblings as good. They were always close.

I try to instill in them, we all we got.

Fee Fee did not remember a lot of positive family memories, but she knew there were happy times even when there was nothing to do but stay in the house.

Fee Fee acknowledged an uncle being there for her and even letting her stay with him for brief periods of time. She felt he understood what she was going through. Fee Fee fondly talked about a lady who mentored her from UWM.

This lady, she went to UWM. She was a doctor of philosophy. She said she was going to take me places I had never been. She introduced me to Pathfinders. She said I can do this and I can do that. I started to jump at stuff. If it wasn't for her, I wouldn't be this well-spoken.

Fee Fee mentioned trying to find her, but her search was unsuccessful.

Placement

Miracles Do Happen

Fee Fee has a very interesting story as to how she ended up in out-of-home care. Fee Fee attributes the reason she was placed in out-of-home care to her mother being sick. However, her younger brother and sister were not initially placed in out-of-home care with her.

I still had my family. It's not that she (mom) didn't want me. She just couldn't take care of me. So I would just leave placements and go home. Why not?

Fee Fee admitted to being hopeful she would have a very short stay in out-of-home care. She had stayed with her dad before, so she assumed she would be placed with her dad right away. However, after her big brother was killed, her dad was unable to accept placement of her. She figured she would eventually end up back home with her mom, but as her mom's health continued to fail, that became less and less of an option. Fee Fee felt abandoned.

Fee Fee struggled as she tried to describe her placements, good and bad.

I was a runner. I never stayed that long. No place was good. Every place was bad. Every time I moved, I thought ... how am I going to get out of here? School was always my excuse. When I left for school, I had options. I would leave for school and never come back.

As she thought more and more about her placements, she did admit to spending one night at a placement. She thought it was "different" because of the curfew and sharing a bedroom with another female. Even though she identified as gay, she liked her own space. She described herself as different from the other girls. She liked to be discreet and by herself. She was in awe that other kids actually went through this and ended up growing up in group homes.

One reason she stayed at this particular placement was because she had made a friend. But after a while this friend got pregnant, and as a result of her pregnancy, her placement was switched. She felt that when her friend left, she had to leave too. Fee Fee opened herself up to this girl because the girl had a secret that she only shared with Fee Fee. She described this girl as always keeping to herself. They had the same MO.

Fee Fee's stay in out-of-home care was halted when she attended a court hearing after being AWOL for a very long time. Even though she was AWOL, Fee Fee still kept regular appointments with her social worker and therapist. They would come and meet with Fee Fee at her mom's house while she was AWOL from her placement. She was so nervous to walk in the courtroom. Fee Fee knew everyone there wanted her to go to jail for going AWOL for so long. However, a miracle happened.

Honestly, it was a miracle. I had been AWOL for so long. I wasn't going to school. And even though I was still seeing my wrap worker and my therapist, I didn't know that was confidential, so they wasn't telling my social worker that they saw me.

When I got to court, they both came on my behalf. My wrap worker and therapist told them I was meeting with them regularly at my mom's house. Not to mention I had a substitute judge and a substitute attorney that day.

My wrap worker and therapist said I'm not a criminal. I'm not getting into trouble. When she leaves her placement, she always goes home. So the judge listened to both of them, smiled, and said, "Congratulations, you're going home!"

Fee Fee was so excited! But she knew there would be a downside. Reunification meant going back to poverty, the projects, and the struggle. Fee Fee said her placements always had the necessities like food, and sometimes they took her shopping. However, as far as reunification, she looked forward to the freedom of being able to go outside. She enjoyed sitting on the porch whenever she wanted, day and night. She appreciated being able to answer the door and answer the house phone.

When Fee Fee returned home to her mom, she found that her mom was still living in low-income housing. Her mother was told that if she accepted Fee Fee back into her care, she would have to move. She was seen as a nuisance by the neighborhood. So her mom moved. Fee Fee lived with her mom for only four months before she died. Fee Fee cried as she told this story.

Fee Fee remembered school being her only "safe zone," especially after her mom died. Her school was always there for her. Even though she was not passing and was failing most of her classes, they were there for her. The school knew her mom was sick and had passed. They tried their best to educate her. She knew they wanted her to succeed in life. They eventually enrolled her in their GED program, and she graduated.

The principal gave me bus fare to and from school. The guidance counselor gave me money so I could eat and helped me get a supplement after my mom passed, so I could live off of for a little while.

The kids didn't know my situation. I didn't get close to people like that. I always felt I was so different from others. Y'all look so brand new. But now that I'm older, I know looks can be deceiving. I always thought … He look nice, so he doing good. I don't look nice, so it's obvious I'm not doing good.

Postplacement

A Lesson Can Be a Blessing

Fee Fee was somewhat appreciative of what being in out-of-home care taught her. Even though her younger brother and sister eventually ended up in the system too, she felt like they had different experiences. Her younger sister went to a group home that was just opening, and the lady really allowed her to have her way. She feels like she understands things her brother and sister still do not understand.

I tell them it can get cold out here. The system was unpredictable, and it can get real bad.

She does not have any ill feelings toward her mother or father because of how her life turned out. Fee Fee learned that no matter who you are and where you come from, you do not have to be a statistic. She repeatedly gave credit to the lady who mentored her from UWM. She feels like her life story would have been much different. The lady from UWM gave her confidence in herself to believe that she could do anything. Also, the day in court when she was reunified with her mom was a self-fulfilling moment in her life.

I look back and say, I handled it. I did that! I can conquer a lot by myself.

Fee Fee did receive her GED, but she has never had a job. She did acknowledge that she always had ways of getting money, which was also why attending school was a struggle. She counted the amount of money she was missing (in her head) while she sat in the classroom. This is why she rarely attended school.

Fee Fee shared an interesting philosophy of homelessness. She was homeless from seventeen to nineteen after her mom passed, but she did not think anyone was aware. She made a point to stay with people for short periods of time, and she never discussed where she stayed when she was not there.

I never gave the person the satisfaction of knowing I was homeless.

Fee Fee feels out-of-home care was not all that bad; it was just not for her. She feels the different placements and people gave her an ability to adapt, which is still something she appreciates today.

She sees out of home care as just another opportunity; you

get from it what you give. She believes there are programs that can really help kids accomplish their goals in life.

Interview #4—"Bee Bee"

I was really looking forward to this interview because she would be my oldest participant so far. We met at her job in her office. The first thing I noticed was her big bright personality. She started the interview by introducing herself as a thirty-one-year-old mom of three beautiful children and a recent college graduate. She described herself as a positive person, spiritually grounded, and very giving.

Preplacement

The Calm before the Storm

Bee Bee was born in Chicago and moved to Milwaukee when she was five years old. Bee Bee had four other sisters, two older and two younger. Bee Bee described her relationship with her mom as very good and said that she was a good mom. Her mom did whatever she could to provide for her five girls. Her mom worked at McDonald's and would often bring the girls there to play in the play land and have ice cream. Bee Bee sees herself as the one who was always protective of her mom. Bee Bee saw her dad here and there, but she did not have a relationship with him because he was not in her life on a consistent basis.

Bee Bee was closest to her older sister, who lived in Chicago. She had her own place, car, and career. Bee Bee saw her as a role model who was living the life she hoped to live someday. She was also very close to her younger sisters. She became closer to them after all three of them were placed in out-of-home care.

Bee Bee also mentioned two uncles she felt close to. And one of her uncle's girlfriends became like family. Bee Bee attributes her family's closeness to her grandmother. Her grandmother would always make sure everybody got together. She was always around.

Placement

Instability and Trauma

Bee Bee attributed her and her younger sisters' placement in out-of-home care to their mom going to jail. She's not quite sure why, but her mom had to go to jail. Her mom was also involved in a domestic violence relationship, and as a result of that, she started using drugs.

I was afraid to ask, but I wanted her to stop doing drugs. Why won't you stop? You know, like do you think about your kids when you're doing drugs? I asked. She says it wasn't necessarily about that. It was more so about just her trying to get high.

Bee Bee did not change placements a lot. The first foster home she stayed in was good. She was so happy she could stay there with her two younger sisters. Still, today she considers that foster mom as one of her heroes. Bee Bee described her as very understanding. She knew her relationship with her sisters was important. She tried to help Bee Bee feel like a normal teenager.

I just wanted to know that my sisters were going to be with me and that we were going to be together because that was the only consistency I had. I was the gatekeeper of my two little sisters. I didn't want anybody to hurt them. I

suppressed a lot of emotions and stuff like that because I didn't want them to see I was afraid.

On the other hand, she was not a fan of group homes. She began to cry as she described her group home experience. When she went to a group home, she got separated from her two younger sisters. (They stayed in the foster home.) She felt there were too many girls living in one house. More importantly, her biggest challenge with group living was how she would deal with her trauma.

I felt like I was being sent to a group home because I had done something bad, and I was like, I didn't do anything. It was a challenge for me because I didn't understand why they (staff) were so angry toward me. It was not a welcoming environment. I mean dealing with trauma, especially teenagers, and if they don't feel comfortable, they are going to lash out.

Bee Bee was eventually placed with her sister in Chicago, but she missed her two younger sisters who were still in out of home care, so she moved back to Milwaukee. All the girls were reunified with their mom for a very short period of time. Her mom lied about her living situation to get the girls back, and when the social worker found out, they were all removed again. Bee Bee knew things did not feel right when they were back with their mom. They moved right next door to a drug house, and her mom began using again. Bee Bee felt that reunification drove a wedge between her and her mom. Here mom told the police Bee Bee tried to stab her and she was sent to detention for two days. She was placed back in a group home where she had previously lived. Mom later told the police and social worker that she made the whole story up. Bee Bee laughed as she remembered this incident.

School was another difficult subject for Bee Bee. She described her school experience as traumatic. She attended more than five different high schools. She felt the people were nosey. She did not think the teachers understood what she was going through. She tried to hide it, but social workers would come up to her school to meet with her. She tried to make excuses and be more discreet. She is still heartbroken over never having the opportunity to attend homecoming and prom. She felt like that would have made her feel like a normal teenager too, but those were things she missed out on. She saw the other kids at school as having normal lives with their moms, who attended parent-teacher conferences with them.

I would go to school. People would ask about, like, your mom. I hadn't had those discussions. You just kind of overlook them or just kind of fancy through them. And I would always have to start over with every new school. Having to go to a new school and meet new people all the time. I was not stable in foster care, and that was detrimental.

Although Bee Bee did not like some placements, she still never AWOLed. She also hated going to court because it was the same old, same old. They would talk about her going home, but she never actually ended up going home. She also hated going to therapy because she felt the therapist would use that as a time to bash her mom. The only thing she might miss if anything was the fact that now she had to pay her own bills.

Postplacement

Don't Let Foster Care Be Your Excuse

Bee Bee was very excited to talk about her life now after out-of-home care. She was so proud of herself and all that she has accomplished despite her time in foster care. Bee Bee described the Independent Living Program as her lifesaver. This program placed her in her own apartment after aging out, which meant she did not have to go back to her sister's house in Chicago. She described her independent living workers as her everything! She had two, a man and a woman.

He was my resource and my go-to person for everything. He took me to set up a bank account. They were really involved in my case. They really helped me stay grounded and not worry. They prepared me for adulthood. She helped me move in, and they took me to the grocery store so I could buy groceries. I had my daughter. I was a teen mom, so that was a challenge for me in itself. And then I was still in high school.

Bee Bee worried as to how she would take care of herself, but she was working and the independent living program paid her first month rent and security deposit. She had several jobs over the course of her life, some while in out of home care (e.g., Taco Bell, the Payday Loan Store, and a bank). Another big accomplishment was graduating from college with a bachelor's degree in human service management. She would not actually consider herself homeless. She referred to it as a transition period where she was jumping from house to house. She did not consider herself homeless because she was in the midst of getting her own place.

Bee Bee talked a great deal about her three children and how the instability she experienced in out-of-home care still affected her today.

And even as an adult now, I feel like okay. I'm not going anywhere. I've been in my house for seven years, and my kids are like, "Can we move?" I'm like, "No! We're staying here." I realize that trauma carried over to my adult life. So the fear of having to move made me unstable in a lot of ways.

Bee Bee had a very direct message for kids in out of home care.

Don't let foster care be your excuse.

Her message for kids in out-of-home care was for them to never give up on their dreams and goals. She reminded foster parents that these kids were not their own but that they should love them like they are. She believed that kids would never forget good caregivers and good placements.

For biological parents, her message was stern. Never forget your job, rights, and duties as a parent even if your child is placed in out of home care. She felt some parents adapted their lives to their kids not being there and then lost the motivation and inspiration to get them back. Instead she felt parents needed to create their lives as if their kids were still there, even if they weren't.

Interview #5—"Dee Dee"

Dee Dee and I agreed to meet at Washington Park Library. The first thing I noticed was her skinny frame and her designer purse and jeans. I even complimented her on her boots and purse. She seemed pleasant.

Preplacement

The Good Life

Dee Dee told a very different story than most kids. Growing up, Dee Dee admitted that she never knew what it meant to struggle. Her mom always provided for her and made sure she had everything she wanted and needed.

Her mom was always her protector. Her mom never put anything past anyone when it came to Dee Dee. She never lived with her dad. She would mostly see him on holidays and birthdays. She remembers that even when she would go spend time with her dad, she would return, and her mom would ask her a bunch of questions about her care. Her mom always wanted to know if anyone did anything to make her feel uncomfortable while she was at her dad's house.

Dee Dee was the only child by her mom. Her dad has another son and daughter. Dee Dee was the youngest of his three children. Dee Dee was close to her brother after her sister moved away to Atlanta. When she turned eighteen, she came back to Milwaukee. Dee Dee and her sister were very close when she returned.

I talk to my sister. I can talk to my sister about anything. I feel she was always going to let me know, but she would listen to how I feel before she would speak.

Dee Dee shared a story about her grandmother. She said her grandmother was on drugs and she had two of her younger children taken away and placed in the system. Dee Dee's mom was one of the kids placed in out-of-home care. Dee Dee was proud to share that her uncle went and got both his sisters from their placement and took care of them. Her uncle got odd jobs to take care of them. One of his jobs was working at the corner store. Dee Dee had a good relationship with her uncle's daughter too.

Dee Dee was very close to her grandfather growing up before he died. His death had a big effect on her because he was always someone she could call on for anything. There were not a lot of kids in Dee Dee's family. They never had family reunions. She described her family in cycles. They would all fight. Someone's birthday would come around, and they would all try to get together. Then there would be another fight, and they would not see one another until the next family member's birthday.

Dee Dee talked about having a strong bond with her pastor. Dee Dee talked about going to church every Sunday, even when she was placed in out-of-home care. She sung in the choir and attended choir rehearsals because the van would pick her up. She tried her best to keep her normal routine.

Placement

Warnings Signs and Red Flags

Dee Dee talked about her time in out-of-home care. Her mom had instilled in her ways to recognize when/if something was wrong. She did not know what to expect when she was initially placed in out-of-home care, but she was confident that she knew how she was supposed to be treated.

She was not sure what her mom actually did wrong, but she knew she was placed in out-of-home care because her mom had gone to jail. Dee Dee's dad was selling drugs, so her mom may have started selling drugs with him, but she was not sure of the whole story.

Although Dee Dee never liked to fight with other kids in out-of-home care, sometimes she was forced to fight. Dee Dee came into out-of-home care with a lot of nice things that her mom had purchased for her as she was growing up. Dee Dee said the girls always stole her personal possessions.

It was messy. I didn't want to fight, but I had to fight over my stuff. I wasn't able to feel confident. I slept with my eyes open.

Dee Dee felt this way in most placements. She would spend the first couple days observing, taking it all in. Eventually, she was in a placement long enough where she felt comfortable. She grew with people, started to feel close to them, and they would talk to each other about their situations.

She liked the group home, but she felt the staff did not know how to handle the messiness. She got tired of the meetings and the talks with the other girls about them stealing her things. The staff could never get the girls to give her things back, so the talks seemed pointless.

Dee Dee would have to resort to AWOLing when things got really bad. Her uncle's daughter would always come and get her, and she would be gone for a couple days and then return. Throughout the entire time in out-of-home care, church continued to be a support and a part of her normal routine.

Dee Dee described herself as introverted while in middle school. However, in high school she tried to open herself up more and become more social. She did not feel changing placements or being in out-of-home care really affected her school because she would always lie about her situation.

I don't like people in my business, so I didn't really say as much to people about my life. In high school, I liked being

closer to people because it was bigger environment. Like I didn't know how to open my lockers, so I needed help.

Dee Dee knew that if she felt that anyone was trying to take advantage of her, she could call her social worker and that she would come.

Dee Dee shared a frustrating story about her aunt. When her mom was released from jail and working to get Dee Dee back, Dee Dee was placed with her aunt until her mom was stable. Dee Dee became emotional as she talked about how neglectful her aunt was to her own seven children.

She got seven kids. They get money from the state. She don't buy them anything. She doesn't have a job. I looked out for them, but what can I do? I tried to help them out because I know what it's like to not feel like someone loves you. She didn't care if they ate, and these are like growing boys. You don't want them to be out here stealing or trying to rob somebody because you're not being the mother you should be.

Dee Dee talked about how eventually everything was on her female cousin to care for the other six siblings. She watched how her big cousin put her life on hold to care for her brothers and sisters. This made Dee Dee dislike her aunt even more. She was happy when her mom got a job and her own place. Dee Dee was reunified with her mom at that time.

Postplacement

Living and Loving

Dee Dee looked forward to moving back in with her mom because she had a good childhood before her mom had gone to jail. The only thing she missed after leaving out-of-home care was the advice she received from some staff. She got a lot of encouragement as she was leaving care. She still kept in touch with some staff and girls on Facebook. She also missed hearing the other girls' stories. She could not believe how some of the other girls had talked about being treated, especially when they had been molested. That had never happened to her. It made her story seem almost insignificant in comparison. She found herself wanting to give them a hug. However, she did not miss having to always fight over her belongings.

Dee Dee felt like most things she already knew, but her mom also helped her prepare for discharge. Mom was doing everything to get Dee Dee back. She apologized for not being there. She had a job, and she got better jobs too. She got a place and eventually got a better place. Dee Dee also graduated from high school and got a job at Taco Bell. She walked into Taco Bell and realized she had the same last name as another girl who already worked there. They were cousins. As a result, Dee Dee was hired on the spot. Before Taco Bell, Dee Dee braided hair to earn extra money. She had watched another aunt braid hair when she was growing up, and she had learned that skill from her.

Today Dee Dee has a nine-month baby girl. She became emotional as she talked about her own child.

I been a mom for nine months, and it's hard. I love my baby for making me a strong person. I couldn't do anything to

get taken away from my baby, like my mom. I don't just buy her stuff. I show her I love her.

Dee Dee has more goals and dreams to be accomplished. She completed high school. She plans to follow in her mom's footsteps by studying nursing in school. Dee Dee is thankful that she has her mom to help her raise her baby. Dee Dee had already finished her CNA classes, and she's been working on her requirements to work in a CBRF. She is also her grandmother's personal care worker. Dee Dee's ultimate goal is to become a pediatrician because she loves kids, but she knows she will have to work her way up.

Dee Dee has never been homeless, but she has been to jail. She was not put in jail, but she was questioned. Her baby's father had hurt a man who was trying to rob them while she was pregnant. The police felt there may have been more to the story, so she was questioned.

Dee Dee's message to kids in out-of-home care is simple. Love yourself!

Whatever happens first and foremost, you have to love yourself. Nobody will love you if you don't, and you just don't care about yourself. I love my life now. I mean, I loved it then, but it was just like a little rough.

Her message for staff and caregivers working with kids in out-of-home care is to treat people how they want to be treated, protect them, and act as role models.

Interview #6—"Lee Lee"

Lee Lee and I spoke over the phone, and she agreed to be interviewed at Atkinson Library. As soon as we walked in the small conference room, she sat straight up in the chair and told me she was ready. She appeared excited about the interview and ready to tell her story. She was originally from Decatur, Georgia. She would be turning twenty next month! She explained how she was biracial, mixed with Korean and African American.

Preplacement

Alone and Abandoned

Lee Lee had no idea who her mom was or where she lived. All she knew about her mom was her government name and social security number.

I could walk past my mom in Pick-n-Save right now and would not know what she looks like. When I was younger, I used to cry about it, but now I've turned out fine. I'm wonderful. I'm great. I'm successful. I thank you for leaving. You made me the person I am.

Her mother gave her away at six months to her great-aunt, but Lee Lee felt she was not so great!

She ended up leaving me with someone else who was like physically abusing me and doing a whole bunch of other stuff, so my school ended up getting involved and reaching out to my father, and that's how I ended up in Milwaukee.

Lee Lee felt her dad saved her when he brought her to Milwaukee to live with him. She always felt close to her dad, even though he was not involved in her life until age eight or nine. She respected her dad a lot for coming to get her.

My father would have gave me the world on a silver platter if I would have asked for it. The time I spent with my dad, he taught me to … in a way, think like a man. He taught me about boys. And I give him a lot of credit for that because ain't nobody to this day who can play me.

Although Lee Lee loved her dad, moving in with him was bittersweet. Back in Georgia, Lee Lee had no siblings. However, when she moved in with her dad, he already had another daughter. Lee Lee was malicious in many ways. She ate her food, started fights with her, and did other petty things to her. Lee Lee was jealous of her sister because she had grown up with both parents. She was happy the relationship with her sister was much better now.

Lee Lee's fondest memory was the time when she moved to Milwaukee and her dad took her to a family reunion in Tennessee. Lee Lee did not know she had such a big family. It was overwhelming. For the first time, she felt complete because she met all types of family (cousins, aunts, and her grandmother's siblings).

Lee Lee felt alone for most of her life, especially before her dad came and got her. She felt close to herself and God, who she learned about at a young age. Lee Lee gave a lot of credit to her school for getting her dad involved.

I didn't even want to come home from school, you know? I didn't really care … if I could live at school, I would have. I felt close to my teachers and my counselors. I didn't even tell them what was going on. I just loved being there because I wasn't at home.

Later in the interview, Lee Lee mentioned that her paternal grandmother being there for her too, but Lee Lee said she also pushed a lot of people away. A cousin was always there for her once she was placed in out-of-home care.

Placement

Bittersweet Memories

The circumstances surrounding Lee Lee's placement in out-of-home care were different than most kids'. Lee Lee placed herself in out-of-home care after leaving Pathfinders. Lee Lee's father was great, but she had already suffered a lot of abuse before she moved to Milwaukee. She had trust issues. In her mind, everyone eventually left, and her dad would too.

I ended up in the system because I had so much hate in my heart. I was mad at everybody. I was angry. I wanted to fight all the time. I just wanted to be bad and malicious and do all this extra stuff.

She talked about a time when she got into trouble at school. To this day, she swears she's innocent and did nothing, but her dad did not believe her. As a consequence, her dad woke her up at 4:00 a.m. to rake leaves. She remembers that was also her dad's birthday. Lee Lee was so upset that she left that day. She ran away to Pathfinders. Her dad tried to come and get her, but she ran away from there. And that is how she ended up in out-of-home care. But it was not at all what she expected.

I was so young and so unknowledgeable on what was going on. I felt like that was better for me. I felt like I'm in the system, ain't nobody gonna tell me nothing, but it didn't go like that. They could tell me whatever they wanted to, and

that's just real. You going to Minnesota. You're moving to Minnesota, and there ain't nothing you can do about it.

Lee Lee had a foster mother who was really nice. She ate well, and she got $60 per week for allowance. Her only issue was she felt like her foster mom treated her biological daughter better than her. But in hindsight, she figured that maybe that was how it should have been. Her biggest concern with placements was if the other girls were cool and whether or not she could have her cell phone. She was still close to one girl she met in out-of-home care. They consider themselves sisters. Lee Lee felt like she really gained a friend in her. They can still depend on each other for different things.

On the other hand, she could recognize when people were in it for the money. She was particularly frustrated with a group home that she went to on her birthday. She was turning thirteen or fourteen, and all she got for her birthday was a cake. She felt like she could have baked her own cake. The staff also took their allowance for the pettiest reasons.

I just felt like they kind of wanted us to be stuck in the system life, and I was not feeling that.

When things got really bad at her placements, she would call her cousin, who would pick her up. Her cousin looked out for her. She knew what type of kid she was. She was not robbing and stealing. She considered herself a good kid who just wanted freedom.

The social worker did not necessarily see things the same way. Lee Lee was eventually placed out of the county in Emery, Wisconsin. There was not another black person in sight. Her grandmother had shared stories with her about how she grew up with racism, so Lee Lee expected the worse.

She laughed and admitted to trying to play the staff. She went into this situation, telling them everything they wanted to hear in hopes that she would be placed back in Milwaukee faster. But the staff saw right through her. They wanted her to be more genuine. Realizing that she really did need the help, she tried to take the program seriously. This was one of the most difficult times in her life because she was taken away from her city and from her family and moved so far that she could not go AWOL.

Postplacement

Stressed but Blessed

As she reflected on her out-of-home care experience, she admitted that she has been blessed. She went from a group home to a foster home and then to her own home. She said that foster homes rarely accepted older girls, but she was lucky to be placed in a foster home the last year before she was discharged. Even rarer was the opportunity to have your own place after out-of-home care, so when the chance came up, her worker encouraged her to take the apartment. Ladelake not only gave her the apartment but also paid the rent while she lived there. They supplied her with dishes, furniture, a TV, and a bed. Lee Lee felt like she learned a lot of things on her own. She had kept a job and a savings account ever since she had turned fifteen.

I love money. I love clothes. I'm one of those girls. My hair, my nails had to be done.

For her, leaving out-of-home care with her own apartment was what she looked forward to the most. She wanted to show people. Most people doubted her, walked out of her life, and did not care. So she wanted to show those people that she was a survivor. She knew she was going to make it with or without family. And she was not going to let growing up in out-of-home care stop her either.

She graduated from high school, and after that, she worked several different jobs. Lee Lee referred to them as the dream jobs that everyone wanted (Foot Locker, Payless, Discovery, Summerfest, and Applebee's). The only time work was a problem was if it conflicted with her school schedule.

Even though she kept a job, taking care of herself after discharge still worried her. Now she would have to go to work every day. So just like her moving in with her dad, she described discharge/aging out as bittersweet too. She knew she had to fend for herself.

Lee Lee became emotional, and she thought about her message to the world.

To parents ... love your kids and don't have kids if you're not ready because when you leave or do bogus stuff, it has a bigger effect than you think.

She talks about still feeling the effects of abandonment from her mother. She encouraged the kids in out-of-home care to make the situation easier, not harder. And to teachers ... pay attention! Her school saved her life when they contacted her dad. Lee Lee plans to return to school when she is able to attend the school of her choice. One day she hopes to become a chef (like her dad). Her dream college is Le Cordon Bleu.

Lee Lee had been homeless in the past, but it did not feel that way at the time. She had a way of identifying certain people to meet certain needs. She would use people for this or that. She's not proud of it today, but at the time she did not care. She slept at her friend's house in the closet, in the park, and sometimes outside on a bus stop. She was proud to say she had never been arrested or gotten pregnant.

Lee Lee ended the interview making it clear that she is not mad at her mom.

Four years ago I probably would have spit in her face. But like now, I'm all grown up. I probably would just hug her. And just be like, Mom, I understand you made a mistake. I would love her. So I would want her to know that I love her regardless of what she did to me. I'm here for her.

Interview #7—"Cee Cee"

Cee Cee and I agreed to meet at Washington Park Library. Cee Cee was short, and she appeared pleasant. She did not seem overly excited about the interview. In fact, she seemed professional as if she were going to a job interview. She carried a small shoulder bag.

Cee Cee was a big talker from the start. She not only answered my questions, but I was impressed with how sharp her memory was. Cee Cee remembered the names of social workers, where she had lived with caregivers, and specific details about events that happened throughout her life.

Preplacement

Pre-Stepdad Era

Cee Cee talked about her family life before her stepdad. Cee Cee remembered life being great when it was just her, her mom, her brother, and her sister. She said her mom worked, and on the days she was off work, they went shopping and out of town, even to Disney World. Her childhood was nice.

Cee Cee's biological father was in and out of jail. However, it was not until she was placed in out-of-home care that the social worker informed her that he had been charged with sexual assault of a minor and domestic violence. Therefore, any visits with him would have to be supervised. Cee Cee found that surprising because he had never hit her mom.

She had daddy daughter days every once in a while, but he was really in and out of her life. She attributed her dad's absence to the fact that every time he and her mom were in the same room, they would argue. So he stayed away, she assumed, to avoid arguments with her mom.

Cee Cee was very close to her siblings and very protective of them too. She would feed them, get them ready for school, and change their diapers. Her younger sister was quiet. She never liked to fight. Cee Cee also talked about the special bond she shared with her grandmother. Her grandmother taught her how to do things like cook and praise dance. She told her to respect her parents and to forgive them even when they were wrong. She remembered songs her grandmother sang to her, getting her hair curled for church, and learning to ride a bike. She enjoyed the time she spent with her grandmother. Still, today she goes to special places they went before her grandma died, such as the park and the lake, just to feel close to her.

Placement

Things Will Never Be the Same

Life changed dramatically when her mom met her stepdad and he moved in. Her mother was twenty, and her stepdad was eighteen. He sold drugs, and even his mother was doing drugs. Cee Cee never got along with him. He was an alcoholic, and he would hit them when he was drinking. Cee Cee just could not understand why her mom was with him and stayed with him for so long.

None of my mom's kids get along with him because you are choosing to be with someone that caused you to lose your kids and you got kicked off of rent assistance.

Her stepdad was the reason all the kids were placed in out-of-home care. Cee Cee described a day that started out like any normal one. Her stepdad got them up and dressed while her mom was in bed. He was getting ready to put her one-year-old brother in the bathtub when she heard him scream. When she got to the bathroom, her little brother had been badly burned. So she called the police. Cee Cee remembered the police showing up quickly and drawing their guns when they entered the house. The police woke her mom. Her stepdad was arrested, and all the children were taken into out-of-home care. Cee Cee figured the school might have also called CPS because they were never there. Later in the interview, Cee Cee disclosed that her stepdad had also been touching her since age twelve.

For Cee Cee, being in the system was better than being home. She has been in more than twenty placements, but she felt like there was one group home that she was always excited to return to.

I like that group home because it was more independent. It was better than other group homes out here. We go on activities, and it's not always skating or the movies or the mall. They took us to do drivers ed, to apply for jobs, and to pay bills. They took in a lot of girls, girls who had been sexually assaulted, girls who were suicidal, and girls that were disabled. They took girls in from off the street.

Cee Cee preferred placements that allowed her to stay with her sister. Similar to growing up, she felt a great responsibility to protect her sister, especially in out-of-home care. She comforted her sister while they were in placements. She did her hair, fixed her food, gave her a bath, and got her dressed. Cee Cee would not allow caregivers to touch her or her sister, and she did not trust the food they prepared. She found her own ways to earn money to buy clothes for her and her sister by doing odd jobs like selling nachos, ICEEs, and popsicles.

She also liked being in placements where she was the oldest. She liked to mentor the younger girls. Cee Cee was also curious as to why foster parents welcomed strangers into their home. She would directly ask them if they did so for the money. She liked one foster mom because she actually explained it to her. She said she was a foster parent because all of her kids were grown and she wanted to help girls have a better life. Cee Cee respected her more for this explanation.

Cee Cee preferred caregivers who were between the ages of thirty to fifty-five. She felt anyone older than fifty-five was too old to deal with a teenager who had issues. She laughed as she talked about the older caregivers she had been placed with.

I don't miss being in foster homes with older people. I can see you placing me with someone thirty on up to age fifty-five, but fifty-five and up, trying to deal with a young female that is a teenager and then they on medication and they got diabetes and asthma and arthritis, and they can't drive a lot.

Cee Cee was not proud to share that with almost every change in placement, there was also a school change. She never had a say in where she moved or where she went to school. Judge would ask her what she wanted, but they never listened. She had several different types of workers—a bureau worker, a wraparound worker, two crisis workers, and a mentor. Early on, Cee Cee felt guilty when placements changed. She wondered what she had done wrong. However, her workers would try to comfort her by saying they just wanted a better placement for her. Cee Cee's desire to remain in any placement became harder and harder the older she got. She remembered staying in one placement for only four days.

Postplacement

Figuring It Out on My Own

The closer she got to adulthood, the more she looked forward to making decisions on her own like going to prom and spending the night at a friend's house. Her bureau worker and therapist decided to have a meeting to plan for her discharge. She was promised her own apartment, but she was never given one. She had to eventually get it on her own.

I liked having my freedom. I was stress-free. I didn't have to worry about arguing with my mom, supervised visits with me and my dad, or me just doing anything. I got to be free. I was glowing. It felt so good to cash my own check. I didn't have to worry about my bureau worker cashing my check and putting it in a safety deposit where I couldn't get a hold to it. I have my own food stamp card. I felt real excited. I am like God. I am becoming a young adult.

Cee Cee missed the sisterhood she had with the other girls in OHC. She felt like they were their own Bad Girls Club. She had fought with and fought for girls while in out-of-home care. She also missed having people to talk to about her problems. She was taught to express herself without using cuss words. She was taught how to cope with her anger by counting to ten, scream-ing in a pillow, and writing poetry.

On the other hand, Cee Cee admitted that she had done a lot of things she was not proud of. She continued to fight with her mom over her stepdad, and now she has no contact with her siblings. Cee Cee cried as she thought about the last two years that had gone by since she had seen her siblings.

Every time I ask her (mom) why I can't see my siblings, she said it's because you are disrespectful and me and you don't get along, but the police always said that don't have nothing to do with your siblings.

After leaving care, Cee Cee had no place to go, so she went to stay with her boyfriend and his mom. Her boyfriend was the only child. His mom had cancer and was doing drugs. Therefore, she had little to no expectations of him. Cee Cee became frus-trated that he was so lazy. He had no job and no education. At the time, she was working and still trying to complete high school, which she never did. She was helping out around the house and helping pay the rent. She tried to air her frustrations to his mom, who had her own issues. His mom became upset and ended up shooting her with a BB gun. Cee Cee was rushed to the hospital, where they found out she was pregnant and was having a miscarriage. After this incident she moved out and was homeless.

Cee Cee was reacquainted with some girls she had previously been in out-of-home care with who were prostituting. They did not encourage her to do what they were doing, but they offered her other ideas as to how she could make money like selling weed and dancing. She started dancing.

After living in hotels and bouncing around from place to place, she did get into an independent living program. She was placed in her own apartment, but there was always a staff person on site. One evening Cee Cee (and two other girls) reached out to her stepdad in an effort to get weed and alcohol. He came to the building where they were staying, and another girl snuck him in. He was not with her mom at the time. He had his own place. They drank and smoked, and he watched them dance. He offered them fifty dollars to go into the bathroom with him, but no one did. Eventually, the staff person heard the noise and saw him enter the building (on the cameras), and he was asked to leave. They said if he didn't leave, they'd call the police. The staff called her mother and told her that the father had been there.

Cee Cee overheard a conversation between her mom and stepmom. For the first time ever, she overheard her mom admit to knowing the whole time about the sexual abuse she endured from stepdad.

She asked him if he was over there trying to get his freak on with those girls. My mom said out loud to my stepmom, who was shocked because she kept telling my stepmom ... he wouldn't touch a little girl. But she said, "Yea, he was and I got him counseling for it." She pointed at me and said, "That's the B that can't get over it."

As Cee Cee reflected on her life and where she was now. She was thankful! Although she was raised by the system, she was a better person now. She was thankful to the people who had worked with her, and most importantly, she was thankful to herself. She is a loving person now who could have been dead or in jail. She is more patient and still uses the resources she learned in out-of-home care (the crisis hotline, shelter hotline, and domestic violence hotline). Cee Cee is planning to start at MATC so that she can earn her last three credits toward her high school completion.

Her message to the world is somewhat complex. She wondered what the world would be like if people had no jobs. She went on to say that people often take things for granted, like their jobs. We do not realize how having a job opens people up to so many other things like insurance and the ability to get from one place to another. Several boys she encountered in OHC have used a lack of employment to justify some of the choices they've made like selling drugs and stealing. When asked if there was a correlation between jobs and out-of-home care, she shook her head yes!

Interview #8—"Kee Kee"

Kee Kee and I agreed to meet at Center Street Library. The first thing I noticed about Kee Kee was that she used one word answers when she introduced herself. I was not sure if she would open up to me.

Preplacement

Protection and Loyalty

Kee Kee said that when she was growing up, her parents fought all the time. Her parents have been legally married for more than twenty years, and they still talk on the phone every now and then. Kee Kee described her dad as saner, even though she thought both her parents were bipolar or schizophrenic when she was growing up. They both did drugs then, and they still do drugs now. Her dad was more levelheaded while her mom had more of a temper.

I've always been a daddy's girl, always, until this day. He is just like a saint from heaven.

Her dad was her protector. He stood up for her when her mother tried to hit her. He gave her money to buy things from the store. When he left, Kee Kee's mom blamed her. However, she always knew her mother had driven him away.

Growing up, her mother wanted her children to fear her. Mom taught her children that eye contact was a sign of disrespect, especially if they were looking at her. Kee Kee remembered keeping her head down to avoid eye contact with her mom. Kee Kee recalled being beaten because she did not wash the dishes the way her mother wanted her to. She felt like she always had to prove her loyalty to her mother.

Around age eleven, Kee Kee jumped in the middle of an altercation between her mom and her new boyfriend. She hit her mom's boyfriend in an effort to protect her mother. Her mother did not see it that way. Instead she chastised Kee Kee for putting her hands on her boyfriend.

Her mom would leave for days. Kee Kee was often left alone at home to care for her younger brothers and sisters.

I was the oldest of seven children. I felt a lot of pressure growing up. Never having a childhood, never being able to play, never being able to do the things I wanted to do because I always had to watch them, take them to the park, feed them, and put them in the bath.

Kee Kee felt her mother should be doing all of these things. She felt close to her brother who was close to her age. He was the oldest boy in the family. She and her brother were both named after their father. They worked as a team in providing care to the other kids. They tried to stick together.

Kee Kee felt a great deal of support from her school.

I had the most perfect teacher in the world, like he helped so much. He braided my hair, gave me clothes, and he was a big influence on my life. People thought he was a pedophile. This man has never crossed the line ... he knows my dad. The principal of the school took me in. She was nice. The problem was that another female was staying there. Like her spot would be taken, because her mama loved me, like literally loved me ... but it was never like I was trying to take her mama. So I moved out of their home.

Other than her school, she felt a bond with her grandmother. Her grandmother often tried to help her understand her parents. Her grandmother felt that neither Kee Kee's mom nor dad was shown love when they were growing up, which made them unaware of how to give love to each other and their own kids.

Placement

Scars Leave Deep Wounds

Kee Kee's mom would always leave for days and say she was going to their dad's house. However, they knew their dad had a girlfriend. This time their mom had been gone for several days. Kee Kee was home alone at the age of nine, caring for her siblings. The youngest was a newborn. The police came to the door, looking for her mother. She had gone to her dad's girlfriend's job to threaten her, and she had busted out all of her windows at work. At first, Kee Kee did not answer the door, but her newborn brother would not stop crying. The police ended up kicking the door in.

They seen the living conditions, and I told them we haven't seen my mom. There's no food in here. She walked up, and

they put her in handcuffs. And they told her that all of us were being taken. She lashed out at me, like, it's because of you. She felt like I should have lied to them.

Her mother blamed her for all the kids being taken away and placed in out-of-home care. Kee Kee felt some guilt over how they ended up in out-of-home care. She understood why her mom did drugs and was mentally unstable, especially after her rights were taken away and her siblings were adopted by her two aunts. Still, she felt a real mother would have been home, doing her job as a parent to prevent this from happening to her kids.

The day Kee Kee was removed, she was sitting in the social worker's office until two or three o'clock in the morning because she wanted to keep all seven of them together, but she was unable to find a placement that could take them all. So they were separated and placed in different foster homes.

Kee Kee loved a group home that she was placed in. They had positive women who worked there. One of the staff took her to church and taught her feminine stuff. She liked how it was structured. Even though they had a curfew, they still had freedom. She felt like they cared. They even let her do extra jobs around the group home to earn extra money. Kee Kee also enjoyed a short stay in respite. She felt this lady was who she would have wanted as a mom if she'd had a choice. She already had five kids staying with her who were younger than Kee Kee.

Kee Kee hated placements when she was the youngest girl in the house. She felt like the older girls were rude and ghetto and would pick on her because she was little. She did not like placements that had a boyfriend or older sons living in the home either.

I don't trust men. I don't put nothing past nobody, so I would never want to stay in a house with a man living there.

Because when I was younger, my uncles played house with me, and I always had to be the mother. They would do things that they shouldn't have been doing.

So when she was placed in these types of placements, she would go AWOL. The judge was not happy with her when she went AWOL from placements that she did not like. Normally, when she would go AWOL, the group home would contact her dad, and he was usually able to get her to return. However, the judge was fed up. So Kee Kee was placed in Port Washington.

She hated this placement. It was the worst experience of her life. She was bullied and beat up for being black. She was molested by her foster mom's husband. She kept calling her social worker, but the woman assumed she was lying. She was not moved until several weeks later. This experience caused Kee Kee to forever see white people differently. She could not understand how people could treat her so badly because of the color of her skin.

Unfortunately, when placements changed, so did her schools. Kee Kee felt like an outcast when she had to come into a new school. Her caregivers wanted her in a school close to their home so that she could take the school bus. Kee Kee tried to stay in contact with teachers who had been supportive and there for her, but it was a struggle to let them know when her placement changed because it happened so frequently.

She felt social workers were at fault. They were untrustworthy. To her, social workers were the most important people in the lives of children. They removed children from homes, and it was their job to make sure they were okay. They should make sure kids are fed and treated well. Social workers rarely cared, so she didn't care either.

Postplacement

Plans and Problems

Kee Kee felt her group home prepared her for her own apartment through Ladelake's Independent Living Program. She was given instruction as to how to budget, but she never fully paid attention. She felt the apartment from Ladelake prepared her for the real world. Soon she would be responsible for finding and funding her own apartment since the program was hands-on. She was not necessarily learning. Now she was doing.

Kee Kee was placed in her own apartment at the age of seventeen. She utilized Ladelake for as long as she could. For the first two years, she was in a program where the rent was free. Then after her time in that program ended, she found another program at Ladelake that paid half the rent for two more years.

Kee Kee felt like the program enabled her. She had a worker who helped her find the house. She went with her to talk to the landlord. They gave her thirty dollars for groceries. She felt like they did everything for her. So she really never took budgeting seriously. This became a big problem when all the services were exhausted and Kee Kee had to find an apartment all on her own.

She got a place with her son's father after Ladelake stopped helping her. But that was not a good idea because the whole time she cared for their son by herself. She became emotional as she talked about how much she had struggled in the past, even to get Pampers for her child while her baby's father just sat there and did nothing.

Kee Kee's son has been a big motivation for her. She finally graduated with her GED at twenty years old. She has worked since she was fourteen years old. Her first job was at Culvers. She worked for Ladelake in the dance club.

She has been homeless several times. Before having her son,

she would sleep outside on bus stops, but after having her son, she got a car. She refused to let her baby sleep outside, so they would sleep in the car. If it was really cold, she would call her baby's father and take her son to his house to stay with him. Her baby's father was living with his mother at that time.

Kee Kee reluctantly talked about a time when she was arrested for stealing money out of the register at Family Dollar. She spent ten hours in jail. She's had other run-ins with the law because of too many parking violations. She always seems to get past these legal issues. She's been able to take classs or fulfill other requirements to avoid jail time and additional fees and charges.

Kee Kee's career aspirations are constantly changing. She has wanted to be a social worker, serve as a police office, and even work in a group home. She would like to help other kids overcome their obstacle now that she is all grown up.

Her advice to kids in out-of-home care is to never give up. She has thought about committing suicide several times, but she feels she has been blessed more because she has not given up.

He sees that you're a fighter. And God is inspired by that, and He blesses you more.

Before concluding, she thanked me for this interview. She felt that it was very therapeutic and that talking was the best way to get over things.

Comparing and Contrasting the Stories and Themes

Preplacement

Surprisingly, even though participants reported not having bonds with parents because of their (physical or emotional) absence, toward the end of the interview, they still expressed the love and continued desire to see them. Participants reported being separated from one if not both parents for a significant amount of time.

My dad. I don't know where he's at. I don't have a real family. Like I don't have no family that's going to be really there for me. I love you, Dad, I want to see you again.

I know there were a lot of different factors. It wasn't just that one. It was, like first of all you're with this person whose not healthy for you. He would never be violent toward us, besides verbal, which is still not good, but he would be very physically violent with my mom. I was always the one who was protective of my mom.

Well, my mother was never there growing up, I never really had a mom. She ended up leaving me with someone else who was like physically abusing me and doing a whole bunch of other stuff. I could walk past my mom right now, and would not know what she looks like. I didn't have my mom; I didn't know my dad at the time. I didn't have nobody. I probably would hug her regardless of what she did to me ... I still love her!

The reasons as to why their mother or father was absent from their lives were all very different—drugs, alcohol, mental health issues, physical health issues, involved in an abusive relationship, or incarceration.

All participants who had siblings reported having a very strong bond with them as they were growing up. Several participants were the primary caregivers for their younger brothers and sisters when their parents were absent.

I can remember time with my brother and sister, but my mom wasn't there. So he always wanted to sleep with me, and she always wanted to follow after me so much (laughing).

I talked to my sister about anything.

Me and my siblings, we got along. I felt close to all my siblings. And I would be protective of all of them.

Consequently, when asked about their fondest memories of the whole family doing something together, overwhelmingly, the participants talked about a memory involving their siblings, but rarely were the parents present.

On the other hand, one participant reported not being close to her half-sister because she was jealous that her half-sister had grown up living with both parents.

Yeah, same father, different mom. You know, I was jealous of that.

All participants reported having a relationship with their grandmother and her presence playing a special role in their lives as they were growing up. The grandmothers were seen as the glue that kept the whole family together, the person everyone revered and respected. They helped these women understand their parents, understand themselves, and understand the world more clearly.

The only other person I had a relationship with was my grandmother. She tried to be there for me.

My grandmother kept us really close together ... grandmas are always usually the one who makes sure everybody better get it together. So grandma was always around.

My grandmother taught me about racism you know, so I was scared. They took me out of my city, away from my family and friends, where I didn't know anybody. My grandma, my father's mom, she was there for me through everything. I would call her. If I needed anything, she was there.

The time these young women spent with their grandmothers was priceless. Their grandmothers were there when they needed them the most, namely while they were young and when their parents were going through difficult times in their lives.

Placement

In regards to OHC, all participants reported their biggest concern was being separated from their siblings. Participants had been caring for their younger siblings their whole lives. Now they were worried that strangers would be responsible for taking care of them.

And my brother and sister been in the system as long as I been in the system, and I don't know where they at. We all got split up, but I remember a little about them. They ain't gonna know me as???? My real name is???? And my adopted name is????

That was my biggest concern because for one, you are not going to take me from my siblings, and I kept saying they only trying to separate us!

I just wanted to know that my sisters were going to be with me and that we were going to be together because that was the only consistency I had. And it was challenging to be there because I was away from my siblings and stuff like that.

This separation amongst siblings was very frustrating and stressful. The participants worried about their safety in their placement, and they worried about their younger siblings who were growing up in a different placement. Participants reported social workers making an effort to keep them together, but these people were often unsuccessful.

In regards to OHC placements, the concerns were all very different (e.g., if the caregivers were nice, if they received a fair allowance, had some freedom, went on outings, and if they felt safe and protected).

I liked that group home because it was more independent. It was better than any other group home out there because they are understanding, they teach young girls, they take us to drivers ed, and they were taking us out to go and apply for jobs. When we go on activities, it's not just skating and movies.

She was the only person who I felt like really stuck to her word. When she said she was gonna help, she would be there. She was the only one I feel that helped me. She didn't ask where I was after AWOLing; all she said was are you okay.

I like how they structured this group home. We were still able to have our freedom even though we had a curfew. Everybody always cared.

All participants reported their placement starting to feel like a family because of the time they were there and/or a special bond they developed with a caregiver or another resident.

I like that group home because it's like they care. It's like family. They take you in, they show you right from wrong, and if you don't like it, they still be there instead of giving up on you. That made me change my ways.

Like they can feel like a family after a while where I don't have to watch my back. Today, like, were still close.

I miss the allowance, having cooked meals, and when I first met "Sarah", I looked at her like a little sister. I was always around younger girls. I played big sister.

However, participants did not like placements that were far away and unwelcoming. They also didn't like if the caregivers seemed to be in it for the money. So too, if the caregivers were male, if they were too old with health issues, or if there was there was no freedom, participates didn't care for the placements then either.

Some pretended to care, but you know I was smart. So I could tell if they're in it for the money. I didn't really feel like they cared about me.

Some placements I didn't like. You catch vibes from certain places. I hated foster homes with old people.

I hated out-of-county placements. I was molested in Port Washington. They hate black people out there. I hated being the youngest because everybody would pick on me.

Participants disliked placements that were out of the county and too far away from their friends and family. Participants also disliked when caregivers used the money they received to provide care for them for their own good. Participants reported their allowance being taken for small things they did.

All participants reported not knowing what to expect when they moved to a different placement. They reported having little to no input as to when they changed placements and where they went.

Group home after group home, foster homes, jumping around. When it first happened, I was nervous, but when it got so frequent, I'd have to change my address and school, meet new staff. I was like, this is getting old. So I felt like I gave up.

I'm ending the placement because I'm leaving. I had an escape plan!

It was just, like here, your moving here, you're going here. And I was like, Well, I don't want to be here. My worker would say, "Well, unfortunately you have to be here!"

Participants gave up the idea that they had any control over placement changes. It did not take long for participants to realize they did not have input as to where they would be placed. All except one participant reported going AWOL from a placement if they were treated unfairly or fighting with another resident.

All participants attributed the emotional difficulty they felt in OHC to them being young, feeling confused, separation from their siblings, and in general, being unable to cope with what was going on.

I had so much hate in my heart. I was mad at everybody. I hated everybody. I just really didn't care. I didn't know much about the system. I was so young and unknowledgeable

about the system. I can do whatever I want, ain't nobody gonna tell me nothing, and it didn't go like that. I was never into none of the bad stuff. I just wanted to be a kid.

I go from bipolar to PTSD and traumatized. I am traumatized! I stabbed my father in the shoulder. My mom allowed my stepmom to beat me. It's hard when you're a kid because you don't know who you want to be with. I was a teenager, feeling like, y'all still have to make decisions for me, like who I can date, if I can go to prom, and spending the night with family and friends. I said I don't want to be in the system no more. I don't know how it might affect my young adulthood because it already affected my childhood. I never had a good childhood.

There was no hope for us! I never know foster parents could be so mean-spirited and racist. Because that doesn't just affect a girl while being there. It could affect your whole life. My attitude is based on you, so if you treat me in that kind of way, do not expect me to show you a good attitude, it's not going to work that way. That's why they're called kids. Because you have to show kids guidance, you have to show them the right way, not just tell them. I went through a lot in my childhood that we didn't know how to cope with.

All participants reported having a social worker while in OHC. Some participants had more than one social worker. Some participants also had a wraparound worker, crisis worker, mentor, and/or independent living worker. The feelings toward social workers varied. Some participants felt like their worker was there for them while others did not feel their worker was there at all.

I've had social workers, crisis workers, and mentors. They tried to give me female workers. I had a worker who was out to get me. At first, I did not like them, but I had to learn that all workers are not the same.

If I ever feel like somebody was taking advantage of me, I knew I could always call my worker, and she would be there for me.

My workers would try to talk to me about my behavior, and we had meetings with my team. The first bureau worker had been with me for two to three years. Then I had to get used to somebody else, almost every two to three months, different workers and different mentors.

Participant's feelings toward social workers varied; however, their feelings about extended family members were consistent.

I wasn't really close to nobody. I always had that mind frame where I didn't care about nothing.

Most of our family members didn't call us, and they didn't check on us. They never did anything.

I kind of resented my whole family to this day because I don't speak to none of them, because I was in foster care, I was in group homes. There were a lot of things I went through that could have been prevented if I was living with my family ... or whatever.

Participants discussed feelings of resentment or disconnect toward extended family members for not being there, while they were in OHC. At one time or another, all of the participants felt alone and abandoned by their extended family members. One participant was unaware of who or where any of her family was because she had been adopted and her name had been changed.

Some participants recalled changing schools when they changed placements, their teachers and kids questioning them about their family, social workers creating a stir coming to meet with them at school, and all the missing days of school (for court and other appointments). For participants who did not change schools frequently, they did admit that when placements changed, their attitude toward school changed.

Participants felt these placement changes caused the educational setbacks. The participants also acknowledged these frustrations toward school, the teachers, and students caused them to get into several fights. Two participants acknowledged that the school was aware of their situation and helpful in some ways (offering a place to stay, getting them clothes, and helping them cope).

I felt close to my teachers and counselors, but I didn't tell them what was going on. I just loved being there because I wasn't home.

I had teachers that would call me a terror when I was a kid getting into stuff. They were all good, supportive and stuff. Like on the weekends, they would check up on me to see how I was doing. And when I go in the system, I was still able to talk to them and hang out with them. Like that moving was messing with my education. I never told any student. They would laugh at you and spread your business. Kids call me a loser, homeless child, saying my mom can't take care of me or saying my mom is on drugs.

I had the most perfect teacher in the world, like he helped me so much. He braided my hair for me and gave me some

clothes. He was a big influence. We actually still talk to this day. He gave me the support I needed and he'd tell my dad when I'm doing stuff wrong. The principal of the school took me in. She was nice. But another female was staying there, like her spot would be taken because her momma loved me. The kids from one of my schools jumped us. I would change schools because the school would be closer to their houses.

Participants reported not wanting other students to find out they were in OHC because of fear this information would be spread throughout the building and they would be teased and ridiculed.

Postplacement

Although the participants were excited about discharge, they were also nervous. The participants had different responses when asked who helped them prepare for discharge and they skills they were taught.

Participants shared a wide range of responses ranging from feeling like they already knew everything (learned on their own) to feeling that they had received some assistance from a social worker (or independent living worker). Some participants reported having a budgeting or money management class (and opening an account).

Obviously, a lot of it was on my own. I've always been good with money management. I've always had a job since I was able to work. I've had a bank account since I was fifteen. Ladelake furnished my whole house. So I didn't need to do nothing, and they was paying rent I was like yeah!

She (Group Home Staff) started to tell me how to set up doctor's appointments on my own, how to go down to the buildings to do stuff on my own, and how to move my mail to other places. She helped me budget and save. She helped me get an account and everything. She helped me grow. She gave me my first house. They wouldn't give me a house at all. They just wanted to give me a list of shelters and bus tickets and send me on my way.

I'll never forget my caseworker because she got me connected to the Independent Living Program and they helped me get a place. My independent living workers helped me stay grounded and not worry. I remember my worker helped me move in and took me to the grocery store. I had a daughter. I was a teen mom. I was still in high school. My worker took me to set up a bank account.

Participants discussed the instabilities they had while being in OHC and how that made them want to be more stable in their adult life (i.e. not wanting to move a lot, wanting the best for their own children, and in general, wanting more out of life).

Although participants reported having negative experiences while in OHC, their message was still positive. They talked about personal regrets and ways they would encourage kids today in similar situations.

Don't take anything you love or long for, for granted. I messed up a lot of opportunities to do stuff and see things from being angry. Do the right thing! If someone is willing to help you, let them.

Don't give up! Don't let foster care be your excuse!

Kids ... trust! Never give up! Forgive!

Participant	Age at Detainment	No. of Foster Homes	No. of Group Homes	Age at Discharge from OHC
1	8	10+	2	18
2	9	8-9	10+	17
3	11	3	4	17
4	13	2	1	18
5	10	3	1	17 1/2
6	14	1	4	19
7	7	12	10	18
8	9	6-7	5	19

Figure 1: Participants' data is organized by age at detainment (initial placement in OHC), number of foster homes, number of group homes, and age at discharge.

Participant	Race	Birthplace	Factors	Reentry	Employed	Did you graduate?	Jail?	Pregnancy	Homeless	What do you miss the most?	What do you miss the least?
1	African American	Chicago	drugs	Yes	No	No	Yes	Yes	No	Allowance	Curfew
2	African American	Las Vegas	Mental issues	Yes	Yes	No	No	No	Yes	Staff/girls	Not getting my way
3	African American	Milwaukee	Health issues	Yes	No	Yes	Yes	No	Yes	Food and shopping	Freedom
4	African American	Chicago	Drugs/jail	Yes	Yes	Yes	No	Yes	Yes	Being taken care of	Court, therapy
5	Black	Milwaukee	Jail	No	Yes	Yes	Yes	Yes	No	Advice	Fighting over my stuff
6	Koren and African American	Georgia	Mom left	Yes	Yes	Yes	No	No	Yes	Being taken care of	Being taken care of
7	African American	Milwaukee	Burned brother	Yes	Yes	No	Yes	Yes	Yes	Allowance/sisterhood	Foster Homes with old people
8	African American	Milwaukee	Living conditions	Yes	Yes	Yes	Yes	Yes	Yes	Being taken care of	Lack of Freedom

Figure 2: Participants' data is organized by race, birthplace, reason for detainment, if reentry in OHC after attempt at reunification, whether or not they had a job, graduated from high school, have been to jail, been pregnant, been homeless, and what they miss the most and least about OHC.

CHAPTER 5

Discussion

Significant Findings of the Study

Understanding Development: Attachment and Separation

FREUD'S INTERPRETATION, WHICH IS BASED ON *DRIVE theory*, explains the development of attachment between mother and infant as a result of satisfaction of the infant's oral and emotional needs through breast-feeding (Brisch, 2002). Contrary to research, the study findings suggest the parent-child bond may not be one of the most significant relationships for the child.

Participants overwhelmingly talked about the importance of their sibling bonds and the daily interactions as a family that made those relationships so important. In some families adolescents act as almost co-parents depending on the needs of the family as a whole. If the development of autonomy in a child (the urge to leave home) threatens to destabilize the family as a whole, the entire family may insist on attachment loyalty (which will inhibit or prohibit the child's separation impulses (Cierpka, 1996; Stierlin, 1980). Consequently, participants struggled with guilt (when placed in OHC). Either they were told and made to feel it was their fault as to why they were removed from their home, or they convinced themselves that they did something wrong and should/could have done something differently.

Bowlby was the first to recognize that childhood experiences—and not just inner psychic forces—affect how an individual responds, develops, and acts. He believed that the "emotional attachments to caregivers were based on social interactions, not on physical gratification" (Mercer, 2006, p. 138). Bowlby concluded that having a committed caregiver is crucial to children's healthy development. Otherwise, the child is vulnerable to a range of threats. Participants in the study reported living with grandmothers, learning things from their grandmother, watching her cook, and going to church. Other than grandparents, participants reported not feeling close to any other family members.

Growing Up in Out-Of-Home Care (OHC)

Doyle (1990) suggested that the abused child looks at removal from the home from three different perspectives—the child as a family member with strong blood ties, the child as a victim (i.e., hostage and kidnap victims), and the child as a victim with an abundance of unsettling emotions. She acknowledges, "Many other youngsters, even those who have been seriously abused, defend their parents, hide their injuries, guard the family secret and try to avoid removal from home." Doyle (1990) refers to this phenomenon as "the paradox of the victim who *resists rescue*" (p. 252).

In regards to OHC placements, participants reported their biggest concern was being separated from their siblings. Bowlby believed that our earliest attachments impact our ability to function socially. Children learn about themselves and how others may respond from the memories of those early experiences. Children suffering from the effects of separation struggle a great deal emotionally. Bowlby proposed that "the sudden loss of a parent or sibling or of care in a succession of foster homes might cause such depression" (Eyer, 1992, p. 62). Participants reported feeling like they had no control over the changes in placement and that they were unclear as to why placements changed, and eventually, the moves caused them to become more upset over time, which made it difficult to form relationships/bonds with new caregivers. Instead they just showed a lot of (displaced) anger.

There are still concerns about lengthy stays children are experiencing in foster care. Henry Maas and Richard Engler (1959) reported the first call against "foster care drift." They found that once children have been in foster care for at least eighteen months, they are likely to remain in care without being returned home or placed in another permanent home. The fact is that most children are likely to *grow up* in foster care (p.421). More importantly, the degree to which a placement was viewed as permanent is associated with children's behavior adjustment (Dubowitz et al., 1993). They found that children whose permanency plans were unclear were at greater risk for externalizing behaviors than were children with clear plans. For example, most adolescents in out-of-home care are rarely concerned about feelings of guilt over certain problem behaviors they exhibit because they see these behaviors as natural reactions to their current situation.

Participants reported suffering a lot of confusion while in OHC because of their age (being young), the lack of daily contact with biological family members, especially their siblings, living with different caregivers, understanding court proceedings, constantly changing placements, and maneuvering through different schools. Hopper and others (2010) described trauma-informed care for individuals as an orientation toward an understanding of trauma to improve the sensitivity of providers and subsequent service delivery. In conducting this research, it is important to assume that participants have been exposed to different variations of trauma, and each participant has coped differently. Recruitment is best if a trusting relationship is established. A safe location should be used to gather data, and ground rules should be explicit, especially regarding participants freedom to stop at any time if the questions become too difficult to answer.

The participants reported some placements eventually feeling like a family and the residents feeling like *sisters*. Social learning perspectives on adolescent development address the importance of modeling, imitation, and identification. With the onset of adolescence, parents and teachers frequently decline as important models, at least in regard to issues and choices that are of immediate consequences (Muuss, 1975). During adolescence it is the peer group and selected entertainment heroes who become increasingly important as models, especially if communication between parents and adolescents breaks down. The feeling of belonging and acceptance can be very important for youth. Youth growing up in the child welfare system are often seeking a place of belonging. They find comfort in other children who have had similar experiences.

Participants reported that school was as unstable as the changes in placements. A consistent finding is that youth in foster care are more likely to drop out of school than those who have not been in care (Courtney et al., 2001). Most of the explanation for these differences is that youth in OHC move from placement to placement and school to school, making it impossible to develop continuous long-term relationships with caregivers and teachers. Eighty percent of children change schools when they change out-of-home placements (Berrick, Courtney, and Barth, 1993), which strains their ability to perform at the same level as other students.

Life after Aging Out

Independent living programs are intended to assist youth in preparing for adulthood, and they may include assistance in obtaining a high school diploma, career exploration, training in daily living skills, training in budgeting and financial management skills, and preventive health activities, among other services. Most importantly, this program encourages youth in foster care to participate directly in designing their own activities that prepare them for independent living and further states that youth need to "accept personal responsibility for living up to their part of the program" (The Federal Independent Living Program [ILP] Public Law 99-272, 1986).

The participants discussed being promised "their own house" when they aged out, and all except three got their own apartment through the Supervised Independent Living Program. Three participants were told that their behavior and choices while in OHC had prevented them from getting their own apartment. So one girl went to live with her mom, one went to live with her boyfriend, and the other one bounced around with different friends and family.

The goal is for all youth aged sixteen or older exiting out-of-home care to leave care with a minimum of the following:

- a driver's license or the preparation for obtaining a driver's license or other access to transportation to school, employment, and other critical activities;

- a high school diploma or GED or enrollment in an educational program designed to result in a high school diploma or GED;
- a written employment history;
- copies of their birth certificate, social security card, and medical records;
- access to funds adequate to support him or herself for a period of three months following exit from care;
- access to and knowledge of local resources, including but not limited to food pantries, human service agencies, health clinics, and mental health facilities; and
- a safe and stable living environment.
  —WI Independent Living Advisory Report, 1999

Examination of Findings that Fail to Support or Only Partially Support the Hypothesis

Surprisingly, though the goal of CPS is preserving the child's well-being, research shows that children who are placed in out-of-home care (OHC) actually have negative life outcomes. The National Research Council (1993) via its Panel on High-Risk Youth concluded that "adolescents who pass through the child welfare system are at high risk of educational failure, unemployment, emotional disturbance, and other negative outcomes ... Adolescents released from foster care fare far worse than either low-income youths or a cross section of the general population" (p. 4). The lack of daily intimate contact with a caregiver causes somewhat of a constant disconnect.

From the data on figure 2, it is clear that these participants reported having some struggles (i.e., maintaining employment, completing high school, avoiding jail, carrying babies to full term, and some moments in life where they were homeless). However, they reported having a number of job opportunities.

They all reported being told about the Independent Living Program (and the possibility of having their own place), and all reported wishing they had done better in school and planning to return to school eventually. For those who had received their own apartment through Independent Living, all except one girl had maintained that same apartment or had acquired another apartment they found on their own.

Limitations of the Study that May Affect the Validity or the Generalizability of the Results

The only obvious limitation to this study would appear to be the small sample size. However, I feel the rich description gives the reader a better glimpse into the feelings, knowledge, and behavior of each participant. Wallen and Fraenkel (2001) explain, "The results of a qualitative study are most effectively presented by means of a narrative, rich in detail also referred to as rich (or thick) *description*" (p. 234). During my study, participants were asked to expand on various stories. The participants were asked to theorize about their lives. Denzin (1989) contends, "Thick description sets up and makes possible interpretation ... and provides the skeletal frame for analysis that leads into interpretation" (p. 101). By this, he means the narrative should present detail, context, and emotion, stimulating feelings that ensure the voices, feelings, actions, and meanings of participants are heard. A rich description enables the reader to transfer information to other settings and to determine whether findings can be transferred "because of shared experiences" (Erlandson et al., 1993, p. 45).

Recommendations for Further Research

Participants reported that the bonds they shared with sib-lings (and how they were formed) were very important to them. Being separated from their siblings was their biggest concern when placed in OHC. The bonds between parents/caregivers and the children are important, and we need to value the bonds the kids have with others family members, especially their siblings. We need to provide opportunities for those bonds to be strength-ened and celebrated, especially during their time in OHC. So too, the placement and school disruptions caused a great deal of (physical and emotional) instability in their lives. Lastly, the participants acknowledge being offered certain things (e.g., a house) after aging out that they may or may not have received for a variety of reasons. (Some reasons were within their con-trol, and some reasons were not within their control.)

Further research is needed on sibling bonds (before, during, and after OHC). Further research is also needed on the experi-ences of young men who were placed in OHC. Do they have sim-ilar experiences as young women? I am interested in research involving the parents (case heads) and extended family mem-bers' reactions, responses, and reasoning.

I am also interested in more research on educational pro-grams that focus on (geared toward and created for) youth aging out of OHC. Do they work? Are the outcomes different for kids in these programs? If so, in what areas are they the most/least successful?

I am interested in doing more research on licensing require-ments, placement requirements, and program requirements for foster parents and group home staff as well as incentives for specific outcomes for kids in OHC.

Implications of the Study for Professional Practice

This study has several implications. First, agencies that license foster/group home caregivers, should consider requiring more training and credentials in trauma-informed care and certain adolescent mental health disorders (causes, medications and reactions, and coping strategies).

Specifically, in regards to sibling groups in OHC, we should offer incentives for placement options that would allow them to stay together. There should be more coordination of services around the sibling group (programs for sibling groups and family therapy with sibling groups).

Everyone, especially the kids growing up in OHC (and their families), need to be better informed and educated about the process. For example, what is the system (OHC)? What happens when you are removed from your family home? What is a social worker's role? What emotions (fears and frustrations) do kids share about OHC? What questions should we ask new caregivers? What are some ways parents and extended family members can help while the child is in OHC? This information should be age-appropriate and mandatory for those placed in OHC. This can be done in a variety of ways, depending on the agency (i.e., age/developmentally appropriate videos/books or some peer-to-peer support/mentoring).

The child placement agencies need to create discussion as to how to minimize the number of placements a child experiences in a given year, and professionals should also discuss their strategies in relation to changing schools too. Every state needs to come up with clear placement and educational goals for youth in OHC.

For youth aging out, we should have more standards/requirements (and offer caregivers incentives when they support youth toward these goals). For example, we could offer reunification with biological family, employment, help with high school and even college work, assistance with drivers ed, accounts showing certain balances (over time), attendance at prom, their own apartment, and/or smooth transition to another program (i.e., the military or job corps). We need to have specific requirements and better tracking so we are supporting youth in working on their goals (and outcomes) earlier in life.

BIBLIOGRAPHY

Administration for Children and Families. "Preliminary estimates for FY 2006 as of January 2008." *The AFCARS Report*
14. Retrieved November 26, 2008. http://www.acf.hhs.
gov/j2ee/programs/cb/laws_polocies/laws/cwpm/polocy.
jsp?idFlag=3.

Anglin et al. *Perspectives in Professional Child and Youth Care.* New
York: The Haworth Press, 1990.

Annie E. Casey Foundation. *Kids Count Data Book: Profiles of Child
Well-Being.* Baltimore: Author, 2005.

Arnett, J. J. "Emerging adulthood: A theory of development from
the late teens through the twenties." *American Psychologist*
55, no. 5 (2000): 469-89.

Barth, R. P. "After safety, what is the goal of child welfare services: Permanency, family continuity, or social benefit?"
International Journal of Social Welfare 8, no. 4 (1999): 244–52.

Barth, R. P. "On their own: The experiences of youth after foster care." Child and Adolescent Social Work 7, no. 5 (1990):
419-40.

Baum, S., and J. Ma. *Education Pays: The Benefits of Higher Education for Individuals and Society.* Washington, DC: College Board, 2007.

Belsky, J. and J. Vondra. "Lessons from child abuse: The determinants of parenting. In *Child Maltreatment: Theory and Research on the Causes and Consequences of Abuse and Neglect,* edited by D. Cichetti and V. Carlson, 153–202. New York: Cambridge University Press, 1989.

Beverley, J. "Testimonio, Subalternity, and Narrative Authority." In *Handbook of Qualitative Research,* 2nd edition, edited by N. K. Denzin and Y. S. Lincoln, 555–65, Thousand Oaks, CA: Sage, 2000.

Bowlby, J. *Attachment and Loss: Volume I.* Attachment, 2nd edition. New York: Basic Books, 1969/1982.

Chase, S. E. "Narrative inquiry: Multiple lenses, approaches, voices." In *The Sage Handbook of Qualitative Research,* 3rd ed., edited by N. K. Denzin and Y. S. Lincoln, 651–79). Thousand Oaks, CS: Sage, 2005.

Chouinard, Michelle. *Children's Questions: A Mechanism for Cognitive Development.* Boston: Blackwell Publishing, 2007.

Clark, H. B., and M. Davis, eds. *Transition to Adulthood: A Resource for Assisting Young People with Emotional and Behavioral Difficulties.* Baltimore: Paul H. Brooks, 2005.

Cook, R. J. "Are we helping foster care youth prepare for their future?" *Children and Youth Services Review* 16, no. 3/4 (1994): 213-299.

Courtney, M. E., I. Piliavin, A. Grogan-Kaylor, and A. Nesmith. "Foster youth transitions to adulthood: A longitudinal view of youth leaving care." *Child Welfare* 80, no. 6 (2001): 685-717.

Courtney et al. *Midwest Evaluation of the Adult Functioning of Former Foster Youth: Outcomes at Age 19.* Chapin Hall Center for Children, University of Chicago, May 2005, 68-70. http://www.chapinhall.org/article_abstract.aspx?ar=1355.

Courtney, Sherry Terao, and Noel Bost. *Midwest Evaluation of the Adult Functioning of Former Foster Youth: Conditions of Youth Preparing to Leave State Care.* Chapin Hall Center for Children, University of Chicago, May 2005, 28-30. http://www.chapin-hall.org/article_abstract.aspx?ar=1355.

Creswell, J. *Qualitative Inquiry and Research Design: Choosing among Five Traditions.* Thousand Oaks, CA: Sage, 2007.

Creswell, J. *Qualitative Inquiry and Research Design: Choosing among Five Traditions.* Thousand Oaks, CA: Sage, 2012.

Davis, A. (1959). "Spearheads for reform: The social settlements and the progressive movement, 1890-1914." Unpublished doctoral dissertation, University of Wisconsin, Madison.

Division of Children and Family Services/Office of Program Evaluation and Planning Out of Home Care Caseload Summary Report (r254, 3/08/07) which is based on data taken from WiSACWIS.

Denzin and Lincoln. *Handbook of Qualitative Research.* Thousand Oaks, CA: Sage, 1994.

Doyle, Celia. *Working with Abused Children.* London: MacMillan Education, 1990.

Dubowitz, H., S. Zuravin, H. Starr, S. Feigelman, and D. Harrington, "Behavior problems of children in kinship care." *Developmental and Behavioral Pediatrics* 14 (1993): 386–93.

Eyer, D. *Mother-Infant Bonding: A Scientific Fiction.* New Haven: Yale University Press, 1992.

Fernandes, A. *Youth Transitioning from Foster Care: Background Federal Programs, and Issues for Congress.* Retrieved from http://www.cafosteringconnections.org/pdfs/CRSReportforCongress.pdf.

Fontana, V. J. *The Maltreated Child. The Maltreated Syndrome in Children.* Springfield, IL: Charles C. Thomas, 1971.

Freud, Sigmund. *Das Ich und das Es,* International Psycho-analytischer Verlag, Leipzig, Vienna, and Zurich, 1923. English translation, *The Ego and the Id.* Translated by Joan Riviere. Hogarth Press and Institute of Psycho-analysis, London, UK, 1927. Revised for *The Standard Edition of the Complete Psychological Works of Sigmund Freud,* edited by James Strachey. W.W. Norton and Company, New York, NY, 1961.

Furstenberg, F. F., R. G. Rumbaut, and R. A. Settersten, eds. "On the frontier of adulthood: Emerging themes and new directions." In *On the Frontier of Adulthood: Theory, Research, and Public Policy.* Chicago and London: The University of Chicago Press, 2005

Haskins et al. *Child Protection: Using Research to Improve Policy and Practice.* Washington, DC: Brookings Institution Press, 2007.

Hawes, J. M. *The Children's Rights Movement.* Boston, MA: Twayne Publishers, 1991.

Jessor, R., and S. L. Jessor. *Problem Behavior And Psychosocial Development: A Longitudinal Study Of Youth.* New York: Academic Press, 1977.

Keating, Daniel. *Nature and Nurture in Early Child Development.* New York: Cambridge University Press, 2011.

Kempe, C. H., F. N. Silverman, B. F. Steele, et al. "The battered child syndrome." *Journal of the American Medical Association* 18, no. 1 (1962): 17–24.

Klaus, M., J. Kennell, and P. Klaus. *Bonding: Building the Foundations of Secure Attachment and Independence.* New York: Addison-Wesley Publishing Company, 1995.

Klee, L., and N Halfon, N. "Mental health care for foster children in California." *Child Abuse & Neglect 11* (1987): 63–74.

Knitzer, J. *Unclaimed Children: The Failure of Public Responsibility to Children and Adolescents in Need of Mental Health Services.* Washington, DC: Children's Defense Fund, 1982.

Krueger, M. *Nexus: A Book about Youth Work.* Washington, DC: University Outreach Press, 1995.

Krueger, M. *Sketching Youth, Self, and Youth Work.* Rotterdam: Sense Publishers, 2007.

Ladson-Billings, G. (1998). "Just what is critical race theory and what's it doing in a *nice* field like education?" *Qualitative Studies in Education* 11, no. 1 (1998): 7–24.

Levy, D. "Maternal overprotection and rejection." *Archives of Neurology and Psychiatry* 25 (1931): 886–89.

Lindsey, D. "Factors affecting the foster care placement decision: An analysis of national survey data." *American Journal of Orthopsychiatry* 61 (1991): 272–81.

Loewald, H. W. "Instinct Theory, Object Relations, and Physic-Structure Formation." *J. Amer. Psychoanal. Assn.* 26 (1978): 493–506.

Lovaas, O. I. "Behavioral treatment and normal education and intellectual functioning in young autistic children." *Journal of Consulting and Clinical Psychology* 55 (1987): 3–9.

Maas, H., and R. Engler. *Children in Need of Parents.* New York: Columbia University Press, 1959.

Maier, Henry. *Group Work as Part of Residential Treatment.* New York: National Association of Social Workers, 1965.

Mercer, Jean. *Understanding Attachment: Parenting, Child Care, and Emotional Development.* Westport: Praeger Publishers, 2006.

Mercer, Jean. *Child Development: Myths and Misunderstandings.* Los Angeles: SAGE Publications, Inc., 2010.

Mitchell, P., and F. Ziegler. *Fundamentals of Development: The Psychology of Childhood.* New York: Psychology Press, 2007.

Muuss, Rolf E. *Theories of Adolescence,* 3rd Edition. New York: Random House, 1975.

National Research Council Commission on Behavioral and Social Sciences and Education. *Losing Generations: Adolescents in High-Risk Settings.* Washington, DC: National Academy Press, 1993.

Nazario, T. *In Defense of Children: Understanding the Rights, Needs, and Interests of the Child.* New York: Macmillan Publishing Company, 1988.

Pecora, Peter J., et al., *Improving Foster Family Care: Findings from the Northwest Foster Care Alumni Study.* Casey Family Programs, 2005. http://www.casey.org/Resources/Publications/Northwest AlumniStudy.htm.

Pecora, P. J. "What works in family foster care." In *What Works in Child Welfare,* edited by M. Kluger, G. Alexander, and P. Curtis. Washington, DC: CWLA Press, 2000.

Radbill, S. X. "A history of child abuse and infanticide." In *The Battered Child,* edited by R. E. Helfer and C. H. Kempe. Chicago: University of Chicago Press, 1968.

Rockhill, Elena K. *Lost to the State.* New York: Berghahn Books, 2010.

Rosenfeld, L. B., J. M. Richman, and G. L. Bowen. "Social support networks and school outcomes: The centrality of the teacher." *Child and Adolescent Social Work Journal* 17, no. 3 (2000): 205–26.

Rothman, D. J. *Conscience and Convenience: The Asylum and Its Alternatives in Progressive America.* Boston: Little-Brown, 1980.

Rudestram, K., and R. Newton. *Surviving Your Dissertation: A Comprehensive Guide to Content and Process.* Los Angeles: SAGE Publications, 2014.

Scott, Brenda. *Out of Control: Who's Watching Our Child Protection Agencies?* Louisiana: Huntington House Publishers, 1994.

Schoeni, Bob, and Karen Ross. "Material Assistance Received from Families During the Transition to Adulthood." In *On the Frontier of Adulthood: Theory, Research, and Public Policy,* edited by Richard A. Settersten Jr., Frank F. Furstenburg Jr., and Rubén Rumbaut, 404–5. Chicago: University of Chicago Press, 2005.

Sears, R. R. "Your ancients revisited: A history of child development." In *Review of Child Cevelopment Research* 5, edited by E. J. Hetherington, 1–73. Chicago: University of Chicago Press, 1975.

Shultz, William. *The Humane Movement in the United States 1910–1922.* New York: Columbia University, 1924.

Sim, K., J. Emerson, K. O'Brien, P. Pecora, and L. Silva. "Postsecondary education and training and support utilization by students from foster care: Findings from scholarship recipient interviews." *Journal of Public Child Welfare* 2, no. 1 (2008): 109–29.

Snyder, T. D., and A. G. Tan. "Beginning postsecondary students." *Digest of U.S. Educational Statistics.* Washington, DC: National Center for Education Statistics, 2006.

Spitz, R. "Hospitalism: An inquiry into the genesis of psychiatric conditions in early childhood." *Psychoanalytic Study of the Child* 1 (1945): 53-75.

Stanfield, J. H., II. "Slipping through the front door: Relevant social scientific evaluation in the people of color century." *American Journal of Evaluation* 20 (1999): 415-31.

Suttie, I. *The Origins of Love and Hate.* London: Kegan Paul, Trench, Trubner, 1935.

The University of Oklahoma, National Child Welfare Resource Center for Youth Development, *The John H. Chafee Foster Care Independence Program: Aftercare Services,* 2003. http://www.nrcys.ou.edu/yd/resources/publications/monographs/aftercare.pdf.

Ten Broeck, E., and R. P. Barth. (1986). "Learning the hard way: A pilot permanency planning project." *Child Welfare* 65 (1986): 281-94.

Ungar, Michael. *Nurturing Hidden Resilience in Troubled Youth.* Toronto: University of Toronto Press, 2004.

US Department of Health and Human Services, Administration on Children, Youth, and Families, Children's Bureau. *Report to the Congress on kinship foster care.* Washington, DC: U.S. Government Printing Office, 2000.

US Department of health and Human Services, Administration for Children and Families, Administration on Children, Youth and Families, Children's Bureau. "Adoption and Foster Care Analysis and Reporting System," 2005. www.acf.hhs.gov/programs/cb/stats_research/afcars/tar/report10.pdf.

US Department of Health and Human, Administration for Children and Families, Children's Bureau. *The AFCARS Report #14: Preliminary FY2006 Estimates*, October 2006. http://www. acf.hhs.gov/programs/cb/stats_research/index.htm#afcars.

Wall, A. E., R. P. Barth, and the NSCAW Research Group. (2005). "Maltreated adolescents: Risk factors and gender differences." *Stress, Trauma, & Crisis* 8 (2005): 1–24.

Wallen and Fraenkel. *Educational Research: A Guide to the Process*, 2nd edition. New Jersey: Lawrence Erlbaum Associates, Inc., 2001.

Weiss, Robert. *Learning from Strangers: The Art and Methods of Qualitative Interview Studies*. New York: The Free Press, 1994.

Winnicott, D. *Primary Maternal Preoccupation: Through Pediatrics to Psychoanalysis*. London: Hogarth, 1956.

Wulczyn, F., and K. B. Hislop. *Foster Care Dynamics in Urban and Non-Urban Countries. Report to the Office of the Assistant Secretary of Planning and Evaluation*. Washington, DC: US Department of Health and Human Services, 2002.

Wulczyn, F., Hislop, K.B., and Harden, B.J. (2002). The placement of infants in foster care. *Infant Mental Health Journal*, 23, 454-475.

Wulczyn et al. *Beyond Common Sense: Child Welfare, Child Well-Being, and the Evidence for Policy Reform*. New Brunswick: AldineTransaction, 2005.

The Child Abuse Prevention and Treatment Act of 1974, Pub. L. No. 93-247, s. 1191, stat. 88 (1974).

The Child Abuse Prevention and Treatment Act of 2010, Pub. L. No. 111-320, s. 2 (2010).

Indian Child Welfare Act of 1978, Pub. L. No. 95-608, s. 1214, stat 3069 (1978).

The Foster Care Independence Act of 1999, Pub. L. No. 106-169, s. 113, stat 1882 (1999).

The College Cost Reduction and Access Act of 2007, Pub. L. No. 110-84, s. 601 (2007).

Housing Choice Voucher Program, Pub. L. No. 106-337, s. 8 (2000).

California Education Code, s. 89342 (1996).

The Federal Independent Living Program, Pub. L. No. 99-272, s. 477 (1986).

Workforce Investment Act, Pub. L. No. 105-220 (1998).

Mentoring Act, 110th Congress (2007–9).

http:www.cwla.org/programs/fostercare/factsheetafter.htm

http://dcf.wisconsin.gov/cwreview/reports/OOHC-Y.htm

http://dcf.wisconsin.gov/children/IndLiving/PDF/Independent Living-rpt.pdf

APPENDIX

Interview Questions: Preplacement

Icebreakers

How are you today?

Can you tell me a little about yourself?

Can you tell me about your biological parents?

Probes

What were your parents like as you were growing up? Where did they work? Which parents did you feel closest to and why? What would have made you feel closer to the other parent?

Can you tell me about life growing up with your siblings?

How many brothers and sisters do you have, including half- and stepsiblings? Who were you closest to as a kid, and why? Was there a sibling you didn't get along with and why? Describe your fondest memory of your entire family together? Can you tell me about your childhood growing up?

What kind of work or chores did you do? What was your least favorite thing to do? What did you do for fun? What was your favorite thing to do? What made you feel sad growing up? Were you ever lonely? Tell me about the other people you felt close to growing up and why (e.g., extended family members, peers, neighbors, teachers, and church members). Were there people you kept your distance from growing up? Why?

Each section specifies the primary questions; however, other probes will develop.

Interview Questions regarding Growing Up in OHC: Placement

Icebreaker

Can you tell me about the day you were first removed from your biological family and placed in OHC?

Probes

How old were you? Why were you removed from the home? How did people react (e.g., parents, siblings, extended family members, peers, neighbors, teachers, and church members)? Can you tell me about your very first placement?

How long were you there? Do you recall the name of a caregiver or the name of the facility? What did you see, think, feel, know, and learn about this placement? How many people were living there? What types of activities did you do there? What were you being told about your parents and siblings? Who were you getting information from? Can you tell me about other placements you have been in?

How many other placements did you have after the initial placement? Do you recall how old you were at the time of these changes in placements? Can you recall the reasons for the changes in placement? What did you expect, think, feel, and learn when moving to a new placement? Can you tell me about the placement(s) you stayed in the longest, and why? Which placement was the shortest, and why? Can you describe your best placement and why. Can you describe your worst placement and why. What caregivers stand out, and why? Were you ever reunified with your biological family? How many social workers did you have? Who was the most memorable, and why? Can you tell me about AWOLing or running away from a placement? Did you AWOL? Why? How long were you missing from the placement? Where did you go? Can you tell me how changes in placements affected your ability to stay connected to your biological family, teachers, friends, etc.?

What (and who) made being in out-of-home care hard, and what (and who) made it easier (e.g., other kids in OHC, extended family members, peers, neighbors, teachers, caregivers, and church members)? What lessons (skills) did you learn while in out-of-home care? Overall, how did being in out-of-home care affect you, your family, siblings, and future outlook on life? What was your impression of OHC?

Each section specifies the primary questions; however, other probes will develop.

Interview Questions regarding Aging Out: Postplacement

Icebreaker

Can you tell me how you prepared for discharge/aging out?

Probes

When were you discharged from out-of-home care (age)? What were the circumstances surrounding your discharge? Who helped prepare you for your discharge, and how? What were you told, by whom, and when? What did you know, expect, think, and feel about being discharged from out-of-home care? How prepared were you for discharge? Can you tell me more about your plans after discharge/aging out and what actually occurred?

Where did you plan to live after being discharged? Whose idea was it for you to go to this place after discharge? What did you know, expect, think, and feel about this new place where you would be living? Who would also be living there? What did you look forward to the most after discharge and why? What were you looking forward to the least after discharge, and why? What was the first thing you did after discharge? Where did you go? Who did you see? What did you do? What skills/resources did you have? Can you tell me about your feelings about OHC now after being discharged?

What do you miss the most about being in out-of-home care (and why)? What do you miss the least about being in out of home care (and why)? Thinking back, do you have any regrets? Was there anything you would have done differently, and why? What would you want to tell children in out-of-home care, your biological parents, extended family members, peers, social workers, and teachers about your experience in out-of-home care?

Each section specifies the primary questions;
however, other probes will develop.

Participants Needed for a Research Study

Aged Out: Narratives of Women who Were Placed in Out-of-Home Care

Requirements

- ✓ Must be female
- ✓ Must be at least eighteen years of age
- ✓ Must have lived in at least one foster home and group home placement
- ✓ Must have already *aged out* of the child welfare system and not be under an existing court order

Each participant

- ✓ will be asked to do one (confidential) audiotaped interview and
- ✓ will be paid $25.00 (cash) for the interview.

Interview locations: the closest Milwaukee public library-conference rooms

Participation in this study is voluntary.

To participate in this study, please
call Lanetta at 414-712-4642.

General questions about the study can be directed to
Lanetta or Gary Williams, PhD at 414-229-5626, UW-
Milwaukee, educational policy and community studies.

Thank you.

CPSIA information can be obtained
at www.ICGtesting.com
Printed in the USA
BVHW080931190620
581580BV00001B/34